Classic Joints
with Power Tools

Classic Joints
with Power Tools

Yeung Chan

LARK BOOKS

A Division of Sterling Publishing Co., Inc.
New York, NY

EDITOR
Andy Rae

ART DIRECTOR AND PRODUCTION
Stacey Budge

PHOTOGRAPHER
Andy Rae

COVER DESIGNER
Barbara Zaretsky

COVER PHOTO
Evan Bracken

ILLUSTRATIONS
Orrin Lundgren

PRODUCTION ASSISTANCE
Shannon Yokeley

EDITORIAL ASSISTANCE
Veronika Alice Gunter
Rain Newcomb
Heather Smith

PROOFREADER
Diane Weiner

SPECIAL PHOTOGRAPHY
Evan Bracken

Dedication

To my wife, Ping, and my two sons, Brian and Wesley. Without their support and care, I would never have had the chance to follow my woodworking dreams and pursue them to a higher level.

Library of Congress Cataloging-in-Publication Data

Chan, Yeung.
    Classic joints with power tools / by Yueng Chan
        p. cm.
    ISBN 1-57990-279-0
    1. Joints (Engineering) 2. Power tools. I. Title.

TA660.J64 C48 2002
684'.083 —dc21   2002016234

10 9 8 7 6 5 4 3 2 1

First Edition

Published by Lark Books, a division of
Sterling Publishing Co., Inc.
387 Park Avenue South, New York, N.Y. 10016

© 2002, Yeung Chan

Distributed in Canada by Sterling Publishing,
c/o Canadian Manda Group, One Atlantic Ave., Suite 105
Toronto, Ontario, Canada M6K 3E7

Distributed in the U.K. by Guild of Master Craftsman Publications Ltd., Castle Place,
166 High Street, Lewes, East Sussex, England
BN7 1XU
Tel: (+ 44) 1273 477374, Fax: (+ 44) 1273 478606, Email: pubs@thegmcgroup.com, Web:
www.gmcpublications.com

Distributed in Australia by Capricorn Link (Australia) Pty Ltd.,
P.O. Box 704, Windsor, NSW 2756 Australia

The written instructions, photographs, designs, patterns, and projects in this volume are intended for the personal use of the reader and may be reproduced for that purpose only. Any other use, especially commercial use, is forbidden under law without written permission of the copyright holder.

Every effort has been made to ensure that all the information in this book is accurate. However, due to differing conditions, tools, and individual skills, the publisher cannot be responsible for any injuries, losses, and other damages that may result from the use of the information in this book.

If you have questions or comments about this book, please contact:
Lark Books
67 Broadway
Asheville, NC 28801
(828) 236-9730

Printed in China

Table of Contents

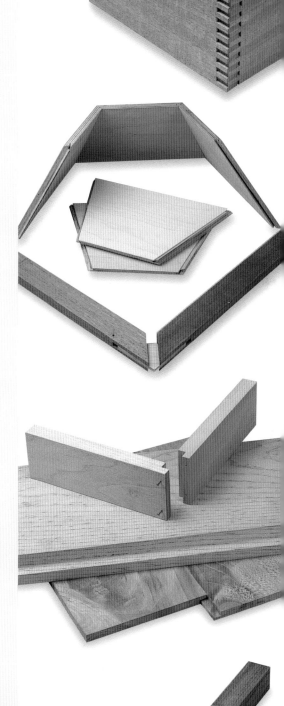

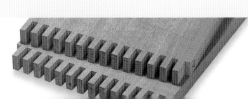

Acknowledgments

I would like to thank the many people who helped transform this book from a daydream into a practical reality.

My editor—plus photographer, furniture maker, and good friend—Andy Rae, supported and championed my original idea, then helped bring my thoughts and words into plain English. He also gave the book a visual boost by shooting the how-to photographs. Great thanks also go to the rest of the staff at Lark Books, from the publisher, numerous editorial assistants, and proofreaders to the talented art department, including illustrator Orrin Lundgren. They have allowed me to share my joinery practices with other woodworkers.

Working with wood and learning the craft of joinery is a never-ending process of practice and improving. As a boy, I grew up in China, where there was a scarcity of instructions, materials, and woodworking tools. After many years of living and working in the United States, I have had the good luck to befriend many woodworkers, and to see their work and share their information and ideas. I've also been able to get my hands on all sorts of woodworking tools and equipment. These opportunities opened new horizons for me, and have taught me more about woodworking than I ever could have imagined. To all my woodworking friends, I express my deep appreciation. And many thanks to the various tool manufacturers who have helped along the way, including Ken Grizzly at Leigh Jig, Chris Carlson at Bosch Power Tools, Vince Caito at Makita Tools, Lisa Gazda at American Clamping, and Richard Wedler at MicroFence.

A personal thanks must be made to my teacher and good friend, Simon Watts, and to Lon Schleining, both for their encouragement. Special thanks to master craftsman Frank Klausz and my woodworking schoolmates Ejler Hjorth-Westh and Willie McArthur, plus many others, for supplying photos of their beautiful woodworking projects shown in this book. I must also acknowledge Jay Heumann, former owner and chief designer of Metropolitan Furniture Company, who gave me the opportunity to learn and improve my machining knowledge and skills, and to learn about furniture manufacturing.

This book is for my master, James Krenov, and his able staff Michael Burns, Jim Budlong, and David Welter; plus all the incredible students who have passed through the gates of the Fine Woodworking program of the College of the Redwoods in Fort Bragg, California over the years. These people pursue the highest workmanship in furnituremaking.

To my parents and my two uncles, who gave me all their love and care.

Foreword

Strong joints are essential in woodworking. But how do you learn the craft of joinery? During my youth in my native Hungary, I had only one option: a long, hard, and often difficult apprenticeship. Modern woodworkers have many less-demanding choices. This book is one of them. Inside, you'll find information distilled from the knowledge of a highly accomplished woodworker, my good friend Yeung Chan.

I have the good fortune to know Yeung on a personal level, and have worked with him at many woodworking shows over the years. He's a good husband, a great father—and an excellent teacher. When I watch him work, I'm reminded of a gypsy playing the violin. What's happening is more than music—it's magic. Perhaps this gift stems from Yeung's welcoming personality and generous and humble nature—but I suspect it has more to do with his origins. The two of us have similar backgrounds. Like me, Yeung Chan came to America from another country—in his case, China—with a hunger to learn and to excel. He has made much from very little. Today, he is a nationally recognized woodworking teacher, and his furniture designs appear in numerous woodworking publications, exhibitions, and private collections all over the United States.

In this book, Yeung dispels the mystery of joinery, making the craft comprehensible, straightforward, and easy to master with the use of simple machinery and lots of shop-made jigs. Using his clear instructions, even a novice can cut high-quality joints quickly and accurately, and with a precision that doesn't require years of study and practice. I salute this woodworker and fellow American for all he has done—and continues to do—for the craft.

—Frank Klausz, February 2002

Introduction

JOINERY is the art of connecting two or more boards together. This technique traces back thousands of years in the East and West, and also in Egyptian culture, where surviving examples of joints in buildings and furniture can be found. What may surprise you is that today's joints haven't changed all that much after many centuries. What has changed is how we make these classic joints.

With today's highly efficient and affordable power tools, you can make the same joints our ancestors made—in much less time, and with much greater accuracy. Precision is an important attribute when it comes to cutting joints. And everyone appreciates saving time. Joints that took our forebears days to construct with hand tools alone can be made by you in a few hours with the right set up and the right machine. This book will show you how.

As much as machines may speed up the process, I believe that modern woodworking is still a balance of using power tools and hand-tool skills. I have two suggestions: please avoid the "do everything fast and quick" approach, a common theme in today's production shops. And don't sacrifice quality for speed. I maintain high standards of workmanship and the highest quality in my own work. That's why you'll always find hand tools, such as planes, chisels, and saws, near my bench. Hand skills provide the details and let you impart great craftsmanship with a personal touch. The result of balancing machines with handwork is great joy and satisfaction—and furniture you'll be proud of.

So please go ahead, look through the book. You'll see all the major joints in woodworking, listed by category. Select a joint that sparks your interest. You'll get an overview of how the joint goes together, its usefulness in furniture applications, and its relative strengths and weaknesses. After that, the choice of machine is up to you. Most of the joints can be made using a variety of power-tool approaches. Pick the machine you're most comfortable with, use the tool you already own, or try a new technique on a new machine.

As a bonus, you'll also discover many jigs and fixtures in the book that work with specific machines. They make the joint-cutting process even easier. Many are useful for other woodworking tasks besides joinery, making them even more valuable in the shop. The jigs I describe and the way I use them result from my own personal woodworking practice; there are many more possibilities and many different methods you can use. I hope my designs inspire you to build even better jigs and fixtures for yourself. After all, a woodworker never has too many jigs.

Making the joints in this book will expand your skills as a woodworker as you learn a variety of joint-cutting methods and procedures. Armed with these techniques, you'll have many possibilities and solutions to help you work on all your future joinery projects. I will be thankful if any of the ideas I describe in this book help you in your furnituremaking.

Power Tools for Joinery

CUTTING accurate joints means using accurate power tools. It pays to invest in good-quality machines, and to make sure you have the necessary accessories, such as blades, cutters, and safety gear to go with them. Here's what to look for:

The Table Saw

The table saw is one of the most-used machines in modern woodworking, and it does an excellent job of cutting joints. There are three types of table saws: benchtop machines, contractor-style saws, and heavy-duty cabinet saws. They function in the same basic manner, and any of the three can be used to cut wonderful joints. The important thing is to make sure your saw is well-tuned. Check that the tabletop is flat, the miter grooves are parallel with the blade, and the fence is accurate.

A good rip fence should be straight, lock solidly to the table, and be parallel to the blade (as well as the miter grooves). If your fence doesn't meet these requirements, buy an aftermarket one. There are plenty of good fences to choose from. I prefer a box-type fence with parallel sides, so I can easily fit shop-made jigs over its square shape.

To cut accurate joints on the table saw, you need a good, sharp blade. There are many kinds of blades designed for

Which Tools Do You Need?

THE JOINTS in this book can be made using any number of machines and power tools. Below is a list of the eight tools I recommend. You don't need all of them. You can select the ones you're most comfortable with, or work with those you already own. With some joints, the procedure might take a little more time depending on the tool being used. However, all of the tools in this book will make accurate joints that will make you proud. In my shop, I use all of these tools for joinery, but they also serve me well for many of my other woodworking tasks. That's because most of these tools can perform multiple chores beyond their intended function. For example, a drill press will drill very accurate holes, but if you mount a sanding drum in the press, you can do light-duty sanding. In the same manner, a router coupled with a fixture can flatten a twisted board, and a biscuit joiner will not only cut slots but make a decent groove as well. Remember, the "right" tool is limited only by your imagination and your resourcefulness.

Table saw	Hand drill
Bandsaw	Drill press
Hand-held router	Hollow-chisel mortiser
Router table	Biscuit joiner

different materials and types of cuts. (See fig. 1.) But for most of my woodworking, especially for sawing joints, I use a premium carbide-tipped blade with a flat-top grind. Because the top of the teeth are ground flat, you can cut a smooth and flat-bottomed saw kerf, an important consideration for joinery work. With this same blade, you can make repetitive cuts to widen a groove. However, when you're faced with making multiple grooves or you're working with a large number of workpieces, it pays to invest in a stacked dado blade. A dado blade will cut grooves, dadoes (grooves that run across the grain of the work), and rabbets, letting you remove more

FIG. 1

SAW BLADE ANATOMY

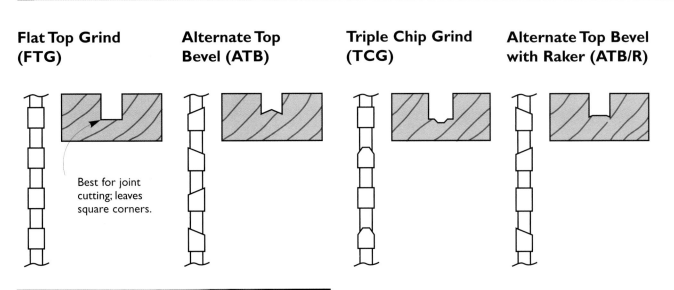

Flat Top Grind (FTG)

Best for joint cutting; leaves square corners.

Alternate Top Bevel (ATB)

Triple Chip Grind (TCG)

Alternate Top Bevel with Raker (ATB/R)

Check by eye. Use a reliable square to check your blade for 90° rather than rely on the saws' stops. Make sure the square's straight edge contacts the saw plate and not the carbide teeth.

wood in a single pass than with a standard saw blade. Look for carbide-tipped teeth, and be prepared to spend more on a quality dado blade than you would on a standard saw blade. Don't forget to keep your blades clean, and if necessary send them out to a reputable saw-sharpening shop.

While it's worth investing in a high-quality blade, even the best blade won't cut accurately if you don't take the time to set it up properly: either square to the table or adjusted to the correct bevel angle. Instead of trusting your saw's 90° miter-angle stops, which are unreliable, it's better to check the blade itself at the table. Before cutting any type of joint, I use an accurate square to check that a blade is truly square to the table, as shown in the photo, left. For beveled cuts, use the same technique, but use a bevel gauge set to the desired angle instead of a square.

A good saw should have several throat plates for different cutting operations. Chances are, the plates that came with your saw are insufficient for the type of joinery you'll make. Luckily, you can make your own plates. The best types of plates are zero-clearance throat plates, which allow only the thickness of the blade to poke through the plate. This minimal clearance allows narrow workpieces to be supported more safely, plus it helps reduce tearout by backing up the cut. Specialty plates, such as those with a wide opening for a dado blade, or plates with angled slots for angled cuts, are worth making yourself. Although most commerical inserts are made from metal, I like to make my plates from a high-quality multi-ply plywood, such as Baltic birch or Finland plywood. After shaping the insert to the opening in the saw, I cover it with plastic laminate for long wear.

One of the best attributes of the table saw is its remarkable versatilty—especially if you equip it with shop-made

Add accessories. A commercial tenoning jig fits most table saws and makes them more versatile, letting you safely hold stock vertically for ripping tenons.

jigs and fixtures. There are several homemade table saw jigs shown in the pages ahead, and they all work to increase your saw's ability to cut a host of joints. In addition, manufacturers have come up with many commerical jigs and accessories that work very well on the table saw. The one to consider for joint-making is the tenoning jig, which lets you cut tenons and other cuts on narrow or tall work safely and accurately, as shown in the photo, above. Tuned up and equipped with a good, sharp blade and well-made jigs and fixtures, a table saw becomes a working system that will provide you with much better results.

The Bandsaw

The bandsaw is another important tool in the shop for joinery work. It can make straight cuts, saw curves, or cut thin and thick stock. It's also an excellent machine for resawing, or ripping thin pieces from thick stock. To make a steady, straight cut on the bandsaw, you'll need a good fence and the right blade.

You can use a stock fence (if your saw came with one), but standard fences aren't usually very tall. In addition, they often mount only to the front edge of the table, making them unstable for heavy cuts. I favor making my own fence, as shown in the photo, below. This fence has a tall and a short side, so you can use either side for different tasks. Two clamps fasten it front and back and you can position it to either side of the blade. (For more on making the fence, see Jigs for Accurate Joints, page 20.) Keep in mind that many bandsaws have a drift angle, or the amount you need to angle the work-piece away from parallel to the blade when making a straight cut. This angle is usually very slight—only a couple of degress—but for accurate joinery, it's a

good idea to determine the exact drift angle of your bandsaw, then set your fence accordingly when you clamp it in place. You can easily check your saw's drift angle by sawing along a marked straight line in some scrap stock, then noting the angle at which the stock must be pushed to keep the cut straight.

The right blade for your bandsaw is an important consideration for making good joints. While you can buy many different types of blades for general cutting, sawing tight curves, resawing, and many other woodworking tasks, I find that a ½-inch-wide, hook-tooth style blade with four teeth per inch (tpi) will perform admirably for almost all my joinery work. For really wide or deep cuts, you can use a wider ¾- or 1-inch blade, which will track straighter. For really tight curves, use a narrow ¼- or ⅜-inch-wide blade.

Similar to the table saw, most bandsaws have stops that register the table at 90° and 45° to the blade. While you can adjust the stops to keep the blade square or at an angle, I prefer the accuracy of using a square or a bevel gauge rested against the blade and the table—the same technique I use when checking my table saw blade.

Homemade fence. This shopmade bandsaw fence is quick to set up and works on either side of the blade. Two sides in different widths add versatility for accommodating large or small work.

Routers, Router Tables, and Bits

Routers have become very popular nowadays—and for good reason. Not only are they proficient at regular woodworking tasks, but they're also incredibly versatile for joinery. A hand-held router can be guided by a bearing-mounted bit, an edge guide, or a fence clamped to the workpiece. Mounted upside down in the router table, a router in effect becomes a mini-shaper, increasing its versatility even further.

Hand-held routers. There are several kinds of routers available to the woodworker, but all of them fall into two broad categories: fixed-base routers and plunge routers. Fixed-based routers accept small or big bits, and consist of a motor armature and a removable base, which allows for easy bit changing. You can find fixed-based routers in straight or D-handle configurations, or use lightweight and highly manueverable laminate trimmers, which accept only ¼-inch shank bits for small cuts. I prefer plunge routers for joinery work. The motor is held permanently to the base, and moves up and down via spring-loaded posts. This movement allows you to make plunge or stopped cuts more accurately than a fixed-based router. And many plunge routers have a micro-adjustment feature that controls bit height in fine increments for a very precise depth of cut, an important feature for accurate joints.

You'll want to invest in a good-quality edge guide to direct your router against the edge of the work for many types of cuts. Many routers come with a decent edge guide, but it's worth looking into a high-quality aftermarket guide that allows for more precise

Edge control. Guiding the router is key to getting good cuts. A standard edge guide (left) works well. An aftermarket edge guide with micro adjustments lets you precisely fine-tune the distance to the bit (right).

control and micro-adjustment of the fence to the bit. (See photo, above.)

A hand-held router—fixed-base or plunge—can be combined with a dovetail jig to rout certain types of dovetail joints, and it greatly simplifies the job, too. For through and half-blind dovetails, look into commerical dovetail jigs. Commerical dovetail jigs employ a guide bushing and special dovetail bits, and they will make very accurate dovetail joints if you take the time to study and practice the setup procedures involved. These jigs are especially useful when you have multiple pieces to cut. Once you set up the jig and the router, the routing procedure is fast and can be repeated. It guarantees great results. (See photo, below.)

Dedicated dovetails. A commercial dovetail jig works with fixed or plunge routers, and saves time when you have multiple pieces to cut. Metal guide bushings and special dovetail bits let you make very accurate cuts.

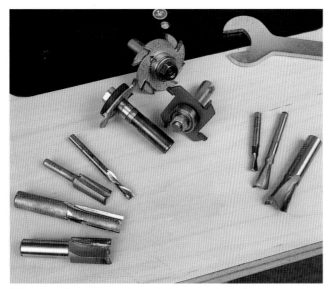

Bits for the router. Essential cutters include (grouped from left to right) straight bits in two-flute or spiral-flute style, slot cutters, and dovetail bits with different angles.

Router tables. While routers in general are designed for hand-held operations, they can easily be mounted inversely under a flat surface to create a router table. Both fixed-base and plunge routers work well mounted upside-down in the router table. One advantage of using a router table versus routing topside with a hand-held machine is that you can move the workpiece, instead of moving the machine. This makes it much easier to rout small or narrow workpieces. And spinning large bits, such as when raising a panel or plowing deep and wide grooves, is much safer on the router table.

There are many great router tables on the market, or you can make your own. (See Jigs for Accurate Joints, page 20.) Your main considerations should be that the top of your table and the fence are flat and straight. Also, the fence should be absolutely square to the table when it is secured. Check it with a square.

Luckily, you'll need only a small selection of router bits for joinery. The key cutters I use are straight bits (either with two cutting flutes, or a spiral-flute, upcut bit), slot cutters, and a selection of dovetail bits in varying slopes, or angles. (See photo, above.) I recommend buying carbide-tipped bits, which stay sharp longer than high-speed steel. And try to buy bits with large, ½-inch shanks if they fit your router's collet. Bits with bigger shanks vibrate less and are stronger, resulting in cleaner, smoother, and more accurate cuts.

Hand Drills and the Drill Press

Joinery often involves making holes, and it's easy to make them with a hand drill or on the drill press. Like routers, it's worth using both types of tools for various joint-cutting tasks.

Hand drills. The modern cordless hand drill has become very popular, although I still use the "old-fashioned" corded variety on occasion. Check that the chuck on your drill is big enough for the largest shank of bit you'll be using. Typical shop drills come with a ⅜-inch chuck, which is usually big enough for most of your drilling jobs; ½-inch chucks are found on bigger, beefier drills. Also, check that the chuck will hold your smallest bits. The jaws on some chucks won't close tightly on bits smaller than about $1/16$ inch, so it's worth investigating your drill if you plan on drilling really small holes.

One of the best accessories for a hand drill is a drill guide. The most useful type of drill guide is a doweling jig. A commerical doweling jig is one way to go, and works by guiding the drill bit precisely at 90° to the work. This lets you make accurate holes for dowels, as shown in the top photo, opposite page. But commerical doweling jigs have their limitations; some can't drill prepindicular holes on a wide surface, while others can't handle drilling into edges. For more convenience and precision, I prefer to make an assortment of doweling jigs fitted with commercial steel drill bushings. (See Jigs for Accurate Joints, page 20.)

The drill press. Like the table saw or the router table, the drill press is a stationary machine that, when set up properly, will make your drilling jobs easy, fast, and more accurate than when drilling by hand. This is especially true when drilling large holes or holes perpendicular to the workpiece.

One area of the drill press that can be improved upon is its table. In most cases, the metal table that comes with the machine is too small for accurate joinery work, especially for long or large workpieces. I increase the table's surface area and expand the press's capacity by making my own table. I also make an accessory fence for accurately registering workpieces. (See Jigs for Accurate Joints, page 20.)

Like router bits, you'll only need a small selection of drill bits for accurate joints. You should size these bits to the dowels you'll be using, and to other joinery hardware such as knock-down bolts and screws. Common dowels sizes are ⅛, ¼, $5/16$, ⅜, $7/16$, and ½ inch, so make sure you have a selection of bits to cover these sizes. My favorites style of bits include three variations: twist bits, brad-point bits, and

Instant dowel holes. A commercial doweling jig is one way to drill very accurate holes for dowels, and is simple to set up and register on the work.

Three types of drill bits. A good selection should include, from left to right, standard twist bits for wood and metal, brad-point bits with clean-cutting outer spurs, and Forstner bits for boring big holes and making overlapping cuts.

Forstner bits, as shown in the bottom photo, left. Twist bits are inexpensive, and will drill into metal as well as wood. For the cleanest cuts, the pointed spurs on brad-point bits enter and exit without tearing the fibers of the wood, so use these bits when the face (and backside) of the workpiece must be blemish-free. Forstner bits are great for drilling large-diameter and stopped holes with flat bottoms. They're also the best choice when you need to drill a series of overlapping holes, such as when drilling out a mortise, since the thin rims prevent the bit from wandering.

The Hollow-Chisel Mortiser

While you can cut wonderful mortises using the drill press or router, you'll need to either square up the mortises or round over the tenons. A hollow-chisel mortiser leaves a distinct, square-ended mortise—an important feature that makes fitting regular square tenons much easier. Instead of drilling or routing a simple round hole or slot, the mortiser holds a square-sided chisel with a spinning bit inside. The bit removes the majority of the wood, while the chisel cuts the outer edges of the mortise absolutely square.

Woodworkers now have a choice of several benchtop models, and many of them are very affordable. One feature to look for on a mortiser is a solid hold-down device that holds the work securely. It's important to prevent the chisel or the workpiece from moving or lifting upwards when you retract the chisel from the wood, since any flex can quickly damage the chisel or tear the workpiece. If necessary, you can use clamps to secure the work.

Regardless of the model of mortiser you select, it's wise to invest in a set of good-quality bits, or mortise chisels, which don't come cheap. A selection of chisels from ¼ inch through ½ inch will cover the majority of your mortising needs. The size of a mortise chisel refers to the square, outside dimensions of the chisel, which in turn corresponds to the width of the finished mortise. (See top photo, next page.)

To make a good mortise, it is important to maintain sharp cutters. Keeping your bits sharp means working on both the drill bit and the chisel. First, I use a fine, cone-shaped stone on the chisel's inner bevel, then I polish all four sides with a fine waterstone, just as I do my regular woodworking chisels. Honing in this manner reduces friction, which makes for a cleaner cut. Be sure to work the drill bit, too. Use a fine file to work the cutting edges until they're sharp.

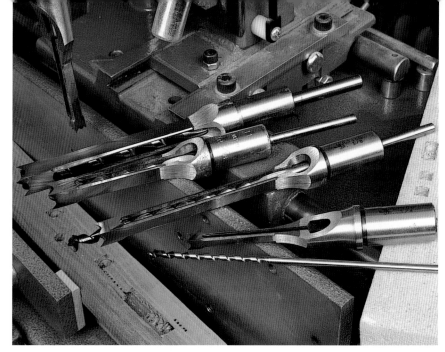

Mortise makers. Mortise chisels cut square-sided mortises, using an inner drill bit to remove the waste while the outer chisel chops the mortise walls. Keep on hand a selection of chisels that correspond to the widths of your mortises.

Equally important as using a sharp cutter is developing good mortising techniques. Always plunge the cutter into the workpiece with a slow and steady feed rate. When you reach the bottom of the cut, pull the cutter out rapidly. This prevents heat build-up, which can burn the wood or—worse— overheat the chisel and the bit inside, which softens the metal and promotes dulling. Always place a piece of wood underneath the workpiece to back up the cut. This helps prevent tearout, and also ensures the delicate cutters don't accidentally contact the metal base.

When cutting a long mortise, establish the two end cuts first, drilling full-depth at one side and then drilling similarly at the opposite side. Then make a center cut. If there's a small web of wood left, align the chisel over its center and plunge straight down. Avoid making cuts right next to a previous cut, since the chisel will want to slide back into the first hole, ruining the mortise or placing stress on the chisel. When making a through mortise, I plunge into the wood from the side where the tenon will exit. This way, if there's any tearout, it will be on the back, or unseen side, of the work and the cheeks of the tenon will cover it.

Wood biscuits. Plate-joinery biscuits are made from compressed beech and are shaped to fit into the slots made by a biscuit joiner. Common sizes are #0, #10, and #20.

The Biscuit Joiner

The modern biscuit joiner has revolutionized joinery, making it possible to produce all sorts of strong, accurate joints in minutes with little or no setup. The machine cuts mating slots in two pieces to be joined, into which you glue wooden biscuits, which act like splines, to secure the joint. These days, you'll find a biscuit joiner widely used in professional cabinet shops and home shops.

The football-shaped biscuits are made from thin pieces of compressed beech, with the grain oriented diagonally for maximum strength and to avoid shrinkage and grain problems. When installed with regular water-based adhesive like white or yellow glue, the moisture swells the compressed wood, making a foolproof and very tight fit. For joinery work, you'll need an assortment of biscuits in different sizes, including #0, #10, and #20, as shown in the photo, below. A good rule of thumb is to use the largest size biscuit possible, without having the biscuit (or its slot) exposed on the outside of the work.

In a pinch, you can forgo a biscuit joiner and cut slots for biscuits on the edges or ends of work with a router and a cutter specially designed for your biscuit sizes. Though not as efficient, this router technique will achieve the same results. There is a limitation, however: A router setup can't make cuts in the middle of a wide surface.

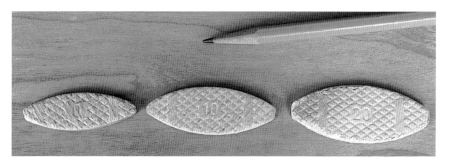

Keep it safe. Wear eye, ear, and nose protection when working with power tools, and use push sticks and featherboards to keep hands clear of cutting edges.

Safety

Regardless of your experience or skill level, accidents—big or minor—can happen. But they don't have to. I believe the biggest danger is when we tune out our minds during repetitive work, forgetting to pay close attention and letting routine get in the way of safe working practices. Having an alert attitude is the first step towards preventing accidents. When we *do* make a woodworking mistake, it causes frustration, and often costs us time and money. The result is that we're not happy, and our frustration won't let us do anything good, let alone cut joints.

The other side of the coin is that when we do it right and with care, things turn out the way we want, we enjoy the working process more, and the result is beautiful projects.

In addition to an intelligent attitude, there are many practical things we can do to keep ourselves safe in the shop. First, dress for success. Remember you're working wood, not getting ready for a party. Avoid loose clothing, tie back long hair, and remove any jewelry. A wrist watch can accidentally snag on tools or workpieces when you least suspect it.

It's always worth spending a few minutes to check your machine setup, then practice the operation without the machine running. The idea is to make sure everything will work properly when you actually turn the switch. This un-plugged rehearsal not only helps you do the job more safely, but also prevents the chance that you'll damage the workpiece or make a mistake.

There are basic safety rules that should become second nature in your shop. The first is eye protection. Always wear safety glasses or shields to protect your eyes from the dust and chips that machines spew in every direction. The same applies when working with hand tools. Hearing protection is another safety must, since most power equipment generates high decibels. Exposure without ear muffs or plugs can cause severe and permanent damage. And keep a dust mask nearby when chips and dust fly. Even with a decent dust-collection system you're likley to see fine dust everywhere. These smaller particles can cause long-term respiratory problems.

To keep fingers and hands safe, use push sticks and hold-down devices whenever possible. I go by the "3-inch rule:" Keep hands away from blades and spinning cutters by at least 3 inches. If you need to come closer, use a push stick. A push stick not only keeps hands clear of the paths of cutters, but often affords more control by letting you push down on the work as well as propel it forward.

Use hold-downs to keep stock where you want it, such as a featherboard clamped to a machine's surface to keep the workpiece tight to a fence or tabletop. And clamp parts securely before drilling or routing. This approach will not only save hands, but can prevent kickback, when the workpiece is unexpectedly and violently whirled or thrown by the cutter—often at you. In many of the photos in this book you'll see guards and hold-downs missing. They've been removed so you can follow the cutting action more clearly. Be sure to use your guards and safety devices when you work.

Basic Hand Tools

▶ **ALTHOUGH** most of the joints in this book can be cut entirely by machines, some of them require a little handwork in order to get a good fit. In addition, good layout is essential before taking the work to your power tool, and checking or laying out angles is one of the tasks you'll face. Some basic hand tools will help you do the job accurately and easily. Hand tools for machined joints fall into two general categories: tools for laying out joints, and tools for cleaning up cuts after machining the workpiece.

My favorite layout tools are simple. For general marking chores, I prefer a mechanical pencil. This type of pencil marks with a fine point, you never have to sharpen it, and the line is always a consistent width even as the lead wears. For an even finer line that also shows up on darker woods such as walnut or rosewood, I use a homemade marking knife with a sharp tip. You can use a simple pocket knife, as long as it's sharp and the tip is pointed. A bonus with knifing a line is that it can't be accidentally erased. For woods prone to chipping, scribing a line prior to machining will prevent tearout. On really dark woods, like wenge or ebony, I make marks stand out clearly by using a white gel pen, which generally leaves a fatter line. These pens are especially useful for labeling and identifying parts, and you can pick them up at art-supply or stationery stores.

Measuring your work accurately is another important layout step. A standard retractable tape measure is always nearby, and a 24-inch steel rule comes in handy for striking and measuring long lines. Marking and measuring for square requires a good square; I prefer 6-inch and 12-inch combination squares, since I can use their marked rules as measuring devices in addition to reading for square or finding 45° angles. For reading and marking any angle, an adjustable protractor and a bevel gauge will cover your needs.

In some cases, a machine's cutter can't reach into some areas of the workpiece, and you'll need to finish the job with hand tools. The marking knife already mentioned works well for these situations. In addition, you'll want a set of quality bench chisels, in sizes from ⅛ inch up to 1 inch wide. I make my own chisels, especially in the narrower widths, and I also use standard bevel-edge chisels. If necessary, you can modify a chisel or knife by grinding it down to the required size. Last, I keep an assortment of files on hand in various sizes and shapes. I occassionally use them for smoothing surfaces, getting into hard-to-reach areas, and for refining joints before assembly.

Hand tools complement machines. A good hand tool kit includes tools for laying out joints, from a mechanical pencil and marking knife to a tape measure, 24-inch rule, squares, bevel gauge, and protractor. Final fitting sometimes requires cutting and scraping tools, such as bench chisels and files.

Jigs for Accurate Joints

Accurate cut-offs. A wooden runner under this single-runner sled rides in the miter groove to the left of the blade, letting you make accurate 90° cuts. Adding an angled fence lets you saw miters.

THE great thing about power tools is they make cutting wood fast and accurate. Jigs and fixtures extend these attributes even further, and it pays to have several in your shop. There are many wonderful aftermarket devices available that you can use with power tools. Even handier are jigs and fixtures you make yourself. Unlike the commercial variety, these jigs can be tailored to solve specific situations and needs, and all of them will help you construct better joints.

In the following section you'll find several jigs and fixtures I've designed over the years that are useful for joinery, grouped by the machines they work with. They also appear later in the book for cutting specific joints. You'll have to size these jigs to fit your particular machine, but most are simple in construction and easy to build, and can be put together with glue and screws or nails.

While shop-made jigs don't have to be fancy, you need to construct them so they are solid and sound, and will hold up over the years. For accuracy, dimension your parts carefully, and use medium-density fiberboard (MDF) or quality hardwood plywood. MDF glues well, comes flat, and stays that way, although it doesn't hold fasteners, such as screws, particularly well. Plywood is stronger, and is usually my first choice for jig material. Some of the best plywood, such as Baltic birch plywood, Appleply, or Finland plywood, is made from multiple plys. Higher-quality plywood is flat and hold fasteners very well. In general, be sure to use ½- or ¾-inch material for your jigs. Thinner panels don't hold screws or nails very well.

Jigs for the Table Saw

As the foremost tool in a woodworking shop, the table saw benefits from a wide variety of jigs designed to make your joinery work easier. You can adapt the following jigs to fit your own saw.

Table Saw Sleds

A table saw sled, also known as a cut-off sled, is a platform that moves over the saw top while carrying the workpiece. This is much more accurate—and easier—than having to push the workpiece, especially with larger work. These sleds register in the table saw's miter grooves via wood runners glued to their undersides. Make sure to fit the runners precisely to your saw's grooves so there's no side-to-side play. This will let you push the sled smoothly past the blade and keep the cut accurate. Also important is some form of grip for your hands. Usually a fence allows you to grab the sled safely, but it's worth adding a block of wood for a handle if you find your hands getting too close to the blade. Remember with table saw sleds that the thickness of the sled itself reduces the depth of cut you can make. However, I've found that a ¾-inch sled lets me cut deep enough for most work.

SINGLE-RUNNER SLED

This sled rides to the left side of the blade. (See photo, top.) Fences screwed to one edge provide hand grips and register the work at 90° to the blade. Work is held to the left of the blade for cutting. Using the sled on its own, you can saw boards to length or cut case parts, such as when squaring the ends of panels. In addition to square cuts, you can make all sorts of angled or miter cuts by attaching angled fences to the jig's base. The gap between the two fences allows for angled work to pass through.

FIG. 1

SINGLE-RUNNER SLED

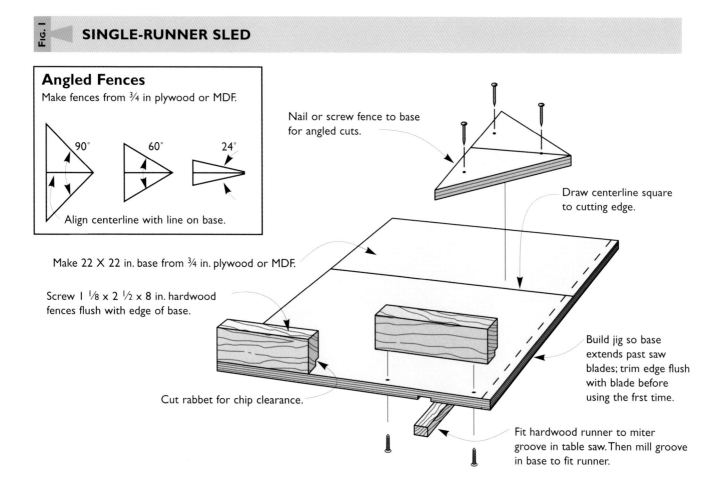

Angled Fences

Make fences from ¾ in plywood or MDF.

90°   60°   24°

Align centerline with line on base.

Nail or screw fence to base for angled cuts.

Draw centerline square to cutting edge.

Make 22 X 22 in. base from ¾ in. plywood or MDF.

Screw 1 ⅛ x 2 ½ x 8 in. hardwood fences flush with edge of base.

Build jig so base extends past saw blades; trim edge flush with blade before using the frst time.

Cut rabbet for chip clearance.

Fit hardwood runner to miter groove in table saw. Then mill groove in base to fit runner.

Bigger cut-offs. Twin runners and a big base on the double-runner sled add stability and let you make bigger cuts, such as when crosscutting case parts.

DOUBLE-RUNNER SLED

If you don't own a miter saw or a radial-arm saw, this sled is a must for general crosscutting. (See photo, left.) While the single-runner sled is convenient for the majority of your joinery work, it doesn't support bigger work very well, such as when cutting in the middle of a long board. In this situation, I use the double-runner sled. Though heavier to lift onto the saw, the sled has a pair of wooden runners and a wider base that extends on both sides of the blade to support large work for safer and more accurate cuts. Tall fences at the front and back of the jig prevent it from being cut in half, even with the blade raised at full height.

I use the double-runner sled like the single-runner sled for crosscutting chores. Plus, I can add the same angled fences for angled cuts. But this sled is also great for making non-through cuts, such as rabbets, dadoes, or other shallow grooves. In addition, the large base provides good support when cutting large panels, such as case pieces. When building

FIG. 2

DOUBLE-RUNNER SLED

Make fences from 1¾ x 5 x 40 in. hardwood. Glue and screw square to base.

Build 27 x 40 in. base from ¾ in. plywood or MDF.

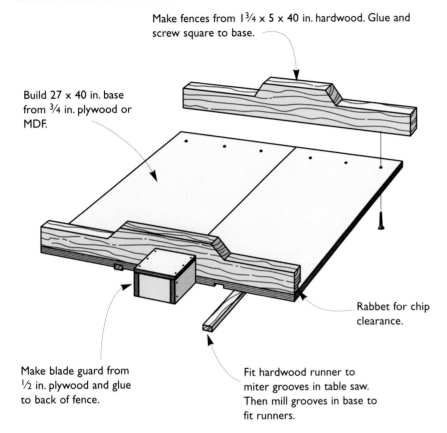

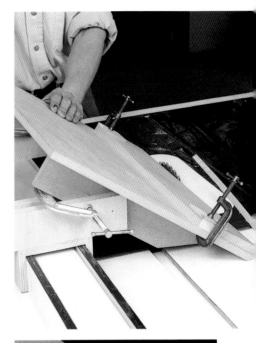

Rabbet for chip clearance.

Make blade guard from ½ in. plywood and glue to back of fence.

Fit hardwood runner to miter grooves in table saw. Then mill grooves in base to fit runners.

Accurate bevels. The adjustable angled fence jig rides the rip fence and allows for very precise bevel cuts without making you tilt the blade (top). Use a bevel gauge to set the adjustable fence to the desired angle, then fasten with C-clamps (above).

this sled, it's important to align the two runners exactly parallel with each other so the sled will move smoothly in the miter grooves. For safety, glue a blade guard to the back of the main fence and in line with the saw blade. You can build a plywood box for the guard, or use a thick chunk of solid wood.

Adjustable Angled Fence

One method for cutting bevels, miters, and other angled cuts on the table saw is to tilt the saw blade to the desired angle and push the stock on a sled or against the rip fence. But angled cuts less than 45° can be difficult or sometimes impossible to accomplish using

this technique, especially on certain brands of saws. This jig addresses this issue by sliding over the saw's rip fence, allowing you to cut practically any angle without having to tilt the blade. A pair of C-clamps holds the fence at the desired angle, which you set using a bevel gauge. Once the angle is set, you clamp the work to the jig and push the entire assembly along the fence and past the blade. In addition to cutting miters, the jig is useful for cutting angled tenons, angled grooves for splines, and compound angles. It's also great for working with irregular stock, such as a five-sided panel that doesn't have any square edges.

FIG. 3 ADJUSTABLE ANGLED FENCE

Make all parts from ¾ in. plywood.

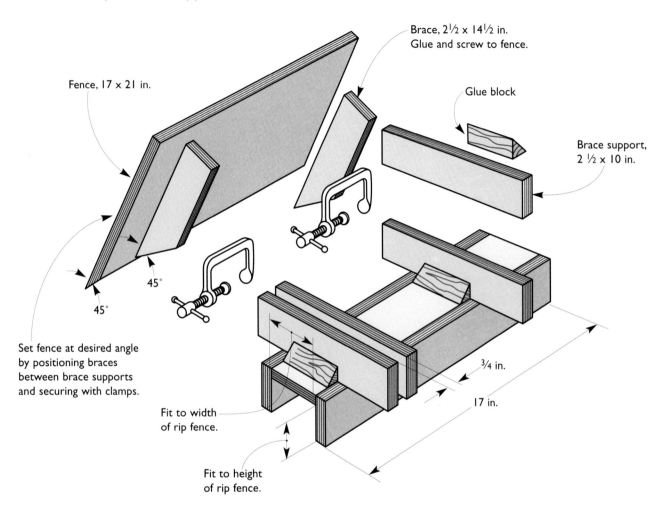

Brace, 2½ x 14½ in.
Glue and screw to fence.

Glue block

Fence, 17 x 21 in.

Brace support,
2 ½ x 10 in.

45°

45°

Set fence at desired angle
by positioning braces
between brace supports
and securing with clamps.

Fit to width
of rip fence.

¾ in.

17 in.

Fit to height
of rip fence.

Tenoning Jig

Much of my furniture is constructed using mortise-and-tenon joints. For fast and accurate tenons, I use the homemade tenoning jig shown on the following page, which lets me rip tenons with a standard saw blade. The jig is sized to fit the rip fence, and slides along it during use. This arrangement lets me use the saw's fence scale to make very accurate adjustments

when lining up the jig and the work to the blade. The stock support holds the workpiece vertically for sawing standard tenons, or it can be removed altogether for cutting angled tenons.

When building the jig, make sure the fence is precisely perpendicular to the table saw top, so your tenons will be accurate. Also important is the stock support, which not only registers the workpiece at the correct angle to the

blade, but also prevents tearout. To keep the stock in good working order, regularly trim its lower end and reposition it when it gets too chewed up to offer solid back-up. With the stock removed, you can clamp workpieces at different positions on the fence to cut different angles, such as mitered tenons. I found that employing a wooden handle adds a measure of comfort and safety not found on commercial tenoning jigs,

and lets me push the jig more easily as it rides the rip fence. You can use an old plane handle for the grip, or copy a favorite tool handle and shape it from scrap hardwood.

Solid tenons. The author's home-made tenoning jig rides the rip fence for stability, and holds the stock perpendicular to the blade (far left). A wood handle (left) offers a secure and comfortable grip.

FIG. 4 ▸ **TENONING JIG**

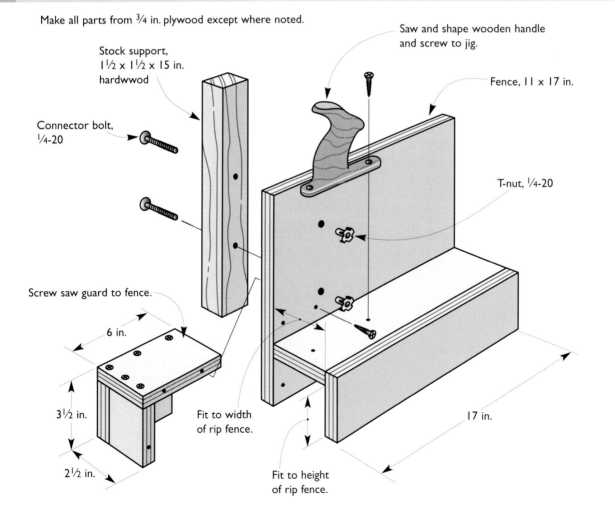

Make all parts from ¾ in. plywood except where noted.

Stock support, 1½ x 1½ x 15 in. hardwwod

Saw and shape wooden handle and screw to jig.

Connector bolt, ¼-20

Fence, 11 x 17 in.

T-nut, ¼-20

Screw saw guard to fence.

6 in.

3½ in.

2½ in.

Fit to width of rip fence.

Fit to height of rip fence.

17 in.

Bandsaw/Drill Press Fence

There are many instances when you need a fence on a bandsaw, such as when making straight cuts or when making identical cuts in several workpieces. If your saw came with a fence, you'll find it handy for joinery work. If you don't own a fence, the quickest and simplest solution is to clamp a piece of wood with a straight edge (a piece of plywood is a good choice) onto the table. Be sure to cut a small ⅛ inch by ⅛ inch rabbet on the bottom edge of the fence so sawdust and chips won't interfere with the workpiece.

For tall workpieces, cuts on the faces of wide work, and for general resawing, I use a larger, shop-made L-shaped fence. The fence can be used in one of two configurations, high or low, by simply turning it 90° to the table. The low side is useful when you need a clear view of the cutting action or when your hands need a better grip on the work; turned 90°, the wider high side supports wide or tall stock. The same fence can be used in either configuration on the drill press, too (see page 34).

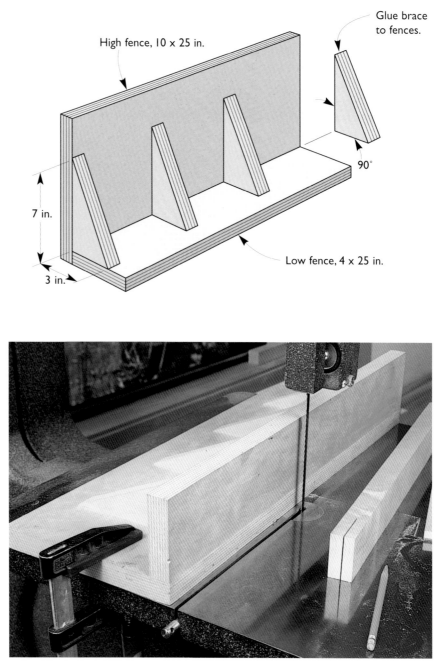

FIG. 5 BANDSAW/DRILL PRESS FENCE

Make all parts from ¾ in. plywood.

High fence, 10 x 25 in.

Glue brace to fences.

90°

7 in.

3 in.

Low fence, 4 x 25 in.

High or low. A shopmade fence offers two working sides in different widths, giving you either high or low fence options to accommodate tall or short workpieces. You can use the same fence on the drill press.

Router Jigs

Like the table saw, the router is a versatile performer when you equip it with a number of router jigs. This category divides itself into three types of jigs: those used with a hand-held router, jigs for the router table, and a dedicated routing fixture for cutting mortises and tenons.

Jigs for Hand-Held Routing

Almost all hand-routing requires some form of guiding edge to control the router, especially when routing grooves or dadoes. The simplest approach for routing dadoes is to clamp a straightedge over the work, then follow the edge of the straightedge with the router's baseplate to make the cut. To simplify this setup and for more precision, I keep two simple jigs on hand. One is designed for cutting straight dadoes and grooves; the other is for angled dadoes.

DADO JIG

This is a handy jig for routing dadoes square across your work, or even at an angle if you desire. A fence guides the edge of the router and a straight bit as you ride the router on top of the base. As the drawing shows, if you make the base a bit wider than necessary, you can use your router and a straight bit to trim the jig with the first cut. All subsequent cuts will fall exactly on this routed edge, assuming you use the same router and bit. This technique makes setup a breeze, since you only need to mark one side of the dado and then clamp the jig to the mark. For square dadoes, clamp the jig square across the workpiece, checking your setup with a square. For dadoes that angle across the stock, clamp the jig at the appropriate angle.

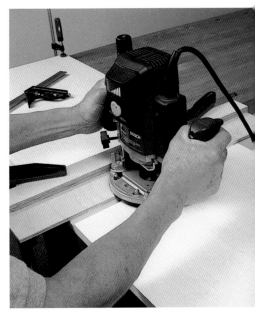

Routing dadoes. This jig is quick to set up because its right edge falls precisely on the cutline. Just clamp the jig right where you need to mill a dado without having to take the router's baseplate into account.

ANGLED DADO JIG

I use this jig and a straight bit in my router when I need to rout a groove at an angle across a workpiece, such as when making angled dadoes. The great thing about the jig is its repeatability: Once you've adjusted the jig to the desired angle, you can quickly cut multiple dadoes in many pieces without having to re-set the jig every time. To rout a single dado, adjust the angle of the jig to your layout line on the workpiece, taking into account the distance from the edge of the jig to the edge of your router bit. Then turn the wing nut to lock the jig at that angle setting, and clamp the jig at both ends to the work. Locking the jig's angle in this manner lets you rout multiple workpieces, too, since you can remove the jig from the first piece without disturbing the angle setting.

 **DADO JIG**

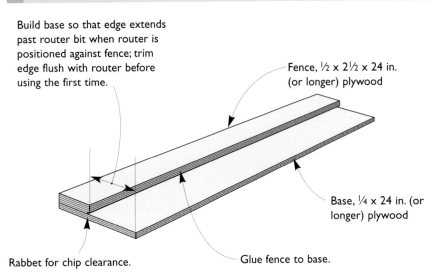

Build base so that edge extends past router bit when router is positioned against fence; trim edge flush with router before using the first time.

Fence, ½ x 2½ x 24 in. (or longer) plywood

Base, ¼ x 24 in. (or longer) plywood

Rabbet for chip clearance.

Glue fence to base.

FIG. 7

ANGLED DADO JIG

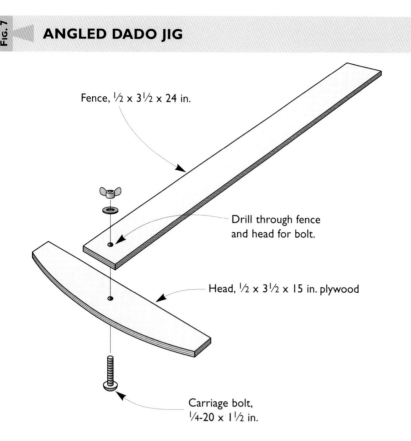

Fence, 1/2 x 3 1/2 x 24 in.

Drill through fence and head for bolt.

Head, 1/2 x 3 1/2 x 15 in. plywood

Carriage bolt, 1/4-20 x 1 1/2 in.

Router Table Jigs

The router table is a versatile performer when it comes to making joints, and you can make it even more adaptable if you equip it with some ingenious jigs. The following jigs not only increase the performance of your router table, but also add a measure of safety and control.

HIGH/LOW ROUTER TABLE FENCE

Every router table needs a great fence, and this one is my favorite. Like any good router fence, it's straight, flat, and square to the table. But it's also versatile. Like my bandsaw fence (see page 25) you can use this fence in one of two modes, either high or low. I use the low side for general routing chores and for increased hand control when working small pieces. The high side supports really wide or tall stock, keeping the work perpendicular to the bit and supporting taller stock with greater safety. To keep things clean, I connect the fence's built-in dust port to my shop's dust-collection system whenever I rout.

Angled dadoes. This pivoting T-shaped jig can be locked to any angle for routing grooves or dadoes, and works great for multiple cuts since you can reposition the device without altering the angle.

It collects dust, too. A built-in dust chute adds to the versatility of this shopmade router fence. Turning the fence 90° provides a taller work surface to support tall or wide stock.

FIG. 8

HIGH/LOW ROUTER TABLE FENCE

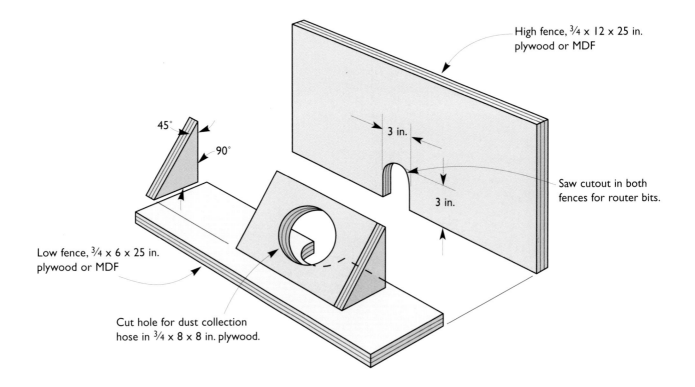

High fence, ¾ x 12 x 25 in. plywood or MDF

45°

90°

3 in.

3 in.

Saw cutout in both fences for router bits.

Low fence, ¾ x 6 x 25 in. plywood or MDF

Cut hole for dust collection hose in ¾ x 8 x 8 in. plywood.

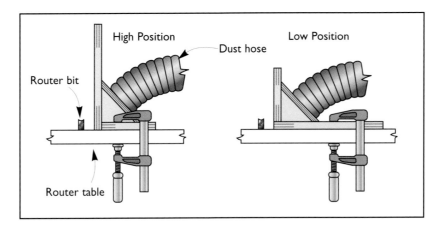

High Position

Dust hose

Low Position

Router bit

Router table

Zero-Clearance Fence

FOR SAFER cutting and better support when routing small workpieces or when working with small-diameter bits, attach a secondary fence over your existing fence to close up the gap. Adding a zero-clearance fence in this manner prevents tearout, supports small, thin, or flexible work, and ensures the work doesn't take an accidental and dangerous dive into what is typically a large opening in your router's existing fence. I use a spare sheet of ¼-inch MDF or plywood for my add-on fence, and secure it temporarily with double-faced (carpet) tape, nails, or clamps. To make a zero-clearance opening for a specific bit, first attach the new fence onto your existing router fence, then secure the assembly lightly to the router table with a single clamp. Use the clamp as a pivot point by swinging the assembly into the spinning bit to cut an exact profile.

Bury the bit. Double-sided tape hold this auxiliary fence onto the existing fence for safer cutting, less tearout, and better support.

FIG. 9 **SLIDING FENCE**

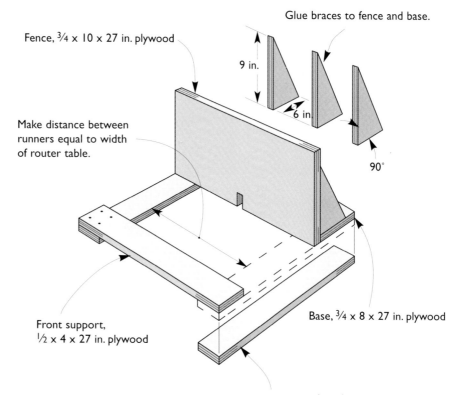

Fence, ¾ x 10 x 27 in. plywood

Make distance between runners equal to width of router table.

Glue braces to fence and base.

9 in.

6 in.

90°

Front support, ½ x 4 x 27 in. plywood

Base, ¾ x 8 x 27 in. plywood

Side runner, ½ x ½ x 22 in. plywood

SLIDING FENCE

I designed this tall, sliding fence for cutting finger joints on the router table, but it's handy for all sorts of specialty routing jobs, such as rabbets, dadoes, or dovetails. It's also good whenever I'm working without a standard fence and need to move the work with great control and at 90° to a bit. The fence has two rails that hug the outside edges of the router table. Before building the jig, make sure your router-table edges are parallel, or the device won't track smoothly and accurately.

A fence that moves. This sliding fence lets you make all sorts of tricky cuts, such as routing box joints or dovetails, that require moving the work at right angles to the bit.

CRADLE JIG

This jig was originally intended for the router table, but I've since found it works just as well on the table saw, and it can easily be moved between the two by adding or subtracting a few parts, as shown in the drawing. The jig lets you make cuts with the work held in the cradle and at 45° to the bit or blade. This feature makes it great for cutting mock finger joints or mock dovetails, although it can be used for numerous other joint-cutting jobs.

The only critical part of the jig's construction is to make sure the two angled fences meet each other at a precise right angle. This way, the square-sided work that you place between the two fences will have firm and solid support.

Cradle your work. By holding square-sided work at 45° to the bit, this jig lets you safely and accurately cut specialty joints, such as mock finger or dovetail joints. It works great on the table saw, too.

 **CRADLE JIG**

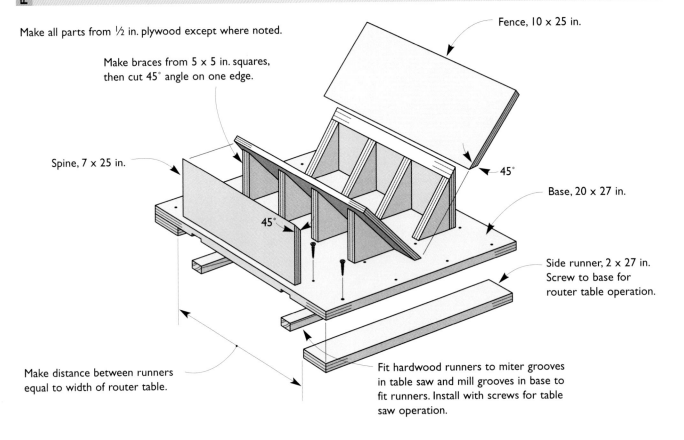

Make all parts from ½ in. plywood except where noted.

Make braces from 5 x 5 in. squares, then cut 45° angle on one edge.

Fence, 10 x 25 in.

Spine, 7 x 25 in.

45°

45°

Base, 20 x 27 in.

Side runner, 2 x 27 in. Screw to base for router table operation.

Make distance between runners equal to width of router table.

Fit hardwood runners to miter grooves in table saw and mill grooves in base to fit runners. Install with screws for table saw operation.

Fig. 11

MORTISING AND TENONING FIXTURE

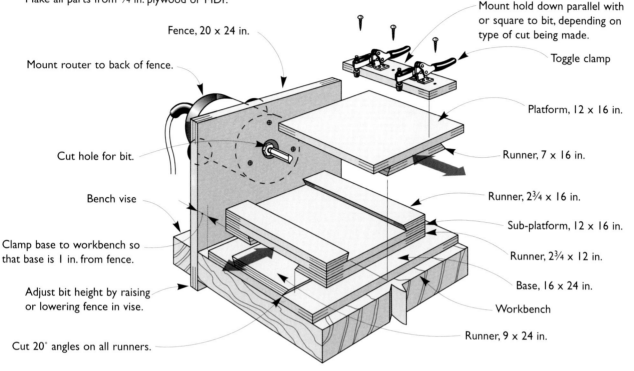

Make all parts from ¾ in. plywood or MDF.

Fence, 20 x 24 in.

Mount router to back of fence.

Mount hold down parallel with or square to bit, depending on type of cut being made.

Toggle clamp

Cut hole for bit.

Platform, 12 x 16 in.

Runner, 7 x 16 in.

Bench vise

Runner, 2¾ x 16 in.

Sub-platform, 12 x 16 in.

Clamp base to workbench so that base is 1 in. from fence.

Runner, 2¾ x 12 in.

Base, 16 x 24 in.

Adjust bit height by raising or lowering fence in vise.

Workbench

Cut 20° angles on all runners.

Runner, 9 x 24 in.

Mortising-and-Tenoning Fixture

This device works with a router mounted horizontally to rout mortises and tenons. It's a true fixture, not a jig, because it becomes a dedicated machine once you've set it up. In fact, it's worth devoting a dedicated router to the device so it's always ready for operation. The fixture works via X, Y, and Z axes, so you get movement in three planes. This allows you to conveniently adjust the bit height, move the workpiece into the bit, and move the work sideways to the bit—the three movements that are key to making mortises or tenons.

To use the fixture for mortising, you secure the hold-down and clamp the work either parallel or perpendicular to the fence (depending on whether you need a side mortise in the edge of the stock or an end mortise in end grain). Chuck a straight bit in the router, and adjust the bit so it projects from the fence a distance equal to your desired mortise depth. Then simply push the work and platform assembly

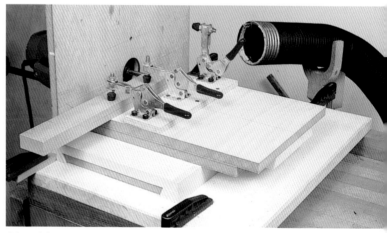

Mortising made easy. This dedicated fixture uses a horizontally-mounted router to cut slot mortises and super-clean tenons. Bit height is controlled by raising or lowering the fence, while two independent platforms move the workpiece into and sideways to the bit.

A jig for every job. The author makes several drilling jigs for specific jobs, greatly simplifying the process of drilling dowel holes. Steel bushings guide the drill bit accurately and provide long wear.

into the bit while moving the sub platform sideways. Make your cuts in ⅛-inch-deep increments to avoid taxing the bit and to get the cleanest cut. Stop when the work touches the fence to rout to the perfect depth. You can clamp stop blocks on both ends of the fence to limit the length of the mortise, or simply pencil stops marks on the fence and use your eye to gauge the correct length. For safety, always feed the work against the rotation of the cutter.

To rout tenons, secure the hold down and the stock perpendicular to the bit, then use the same technique as when routing an end mortise. Be sure to rout each side of the stock to form a perfectly centered tenon, and make your cuts in small increments. Again, always move the work against the rotation of the bit.

Drilling Jigs

In furnituremaking, locating holes accurately is important, for example, when drilling pilot holes for fasteners or shelf hardware. The same is true when boring holes for joints, such as for dowels. If you drill the holes in the wrong place, parts won't align with each other or won't fit together, and you'll have trouble during assembly. The end result will reflect poor workmanship. Whether you're drilling by hand or using the drill press, you'll need some form of a guide so your holes are precisely perpendicular to the work and are properly located. There are several drilling jigs you can build that will make all your hole boring chores accurate.

FIG. 12

DOWELING JIGS

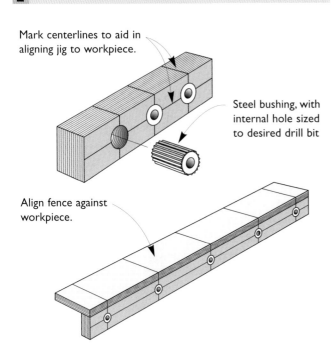

Mark centerlines to aid in aligning jig to workpiece.

Steel bushing, with internal hole sized to desired drill bit

Align fence against workpiece.

pieces or align with reference lines that I mark on the stock. And these jigs are designed to last. The metal bushings allow you to use the jigs over and over without wearing out their accuracy. Bushings are available from industrial-supply stores and catalogs; buy them to fit the particular diameter of bit you're using. I find the most common sizes for my work are $1/4$, $5/16$, $3/8$, and $1/2$ inch.

Drill Press Jigs

The drill press is a wonderful machine for drilling very accurate holes that are perfectly perpendicular to your work. But you can add a couple of shop-made accessories that will greatly increase the versatility and precision of the drill press.

Doweling Jigs

To drill dowel holes accurately, they must be spaced evenly between mating pieces, and they should be accurately centered on the stock's thickness. The answer is to use a doweling jig, which works with a hand drill to guide the drill bit precisely where you want it to go. Commercial doweling jigs are great and will help do the job admirably (see page 15). But commercial jigs have their limitations. Some are designed only for end or edge boring, and some allow you to drill holes only in the face of your work. Plus, the number of guide holes are limited and hole centers are set to specific distances, which can slow down the drilling process and force you to relocate the jig a number of times, especially on large drilling jobs.

For more versatility and more precise holes, I prefer to use an assortment of homemade doweling jigs fitted with commercial steel drill bushings. You can make the jigs to suit particular jobs and use them over and over, or build several so you're equipped for every drilling operation you can imagine. Plus, making your own dedicated doweling jigs gives you pre-set dimensions, which means setup is easy. To keep things simple, most of my jigs reference on the edges of my work-

Align and drill. Center the jig's mark over a centermark on your work and use masking tape on the bit to gauge the correct hole depth.

Deep drilling. This shopmade fence can be clamped in the conventional manner atop the drill press table, or stood on end for drilling into long work.

DRILL PRESS/BANDSAW FENCE

There are many times when we need to reference our work against a fence clamped to the drill press table, such as when drilling a series of parallel holes or when boring holes in multiple parts. For the quickest and easiest setup, you can clamp a straightedge to the table, made from any material with a straight edge, such as a jointed board or a piece of plywood. For accuracy, mill a small rabbet on the bottom edge of the fence to clear chips and wayward debris.

A more versatile fence is the same exact fence I use on the bandsaw (see page 25), which works equally well on the drill press table. You can use the fence in a high or low position, which gives you plenty of options for referencing workpieces in different orientations. Another good use for this fence is mounting it in a vertical position for holding work parallel to the bit. This arrangement lets you drill vertical holes, such as when drilling into the end of a rail for dowels.

Deluxe table. This wide and deep plywood table adds good support for large jobs, and its replaceable insert provides a solid surface that prevents tearout when drilling through stock.

DRILL PRESS TABLE

Most home-shop drill presses come with inadequate tables. I find the typical table doesn't provide enough support in many drilling situations, and the metal surface is risky to bits should you ever accidentally drill into it. To overcome these drawbacks, I use a secondary table made from plywood that slips over the top of my existing table.

The large top gives good support and provides plenty of clamping area so you can secure workpieces safely. The table has a removable insert, which helps reduce tearout on the underside of the work. When one side of the insert gets so full of holes that it starts to resemble Swiss cheese, either flip it over or toss it and replace it with a fresh one.

FIG. 13 ◄ **DRILL PRESS TABLE**

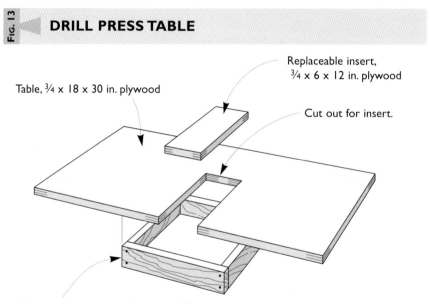

Table, ¾ x 18 x 30 in. plywood

Replaceable insert, ¾ x 6 x 12 in. plywood

Cut out for insert.

Fit wood frame around existing drill press table, then glue and screw to underside of plywood table.

Preparation and Assembly

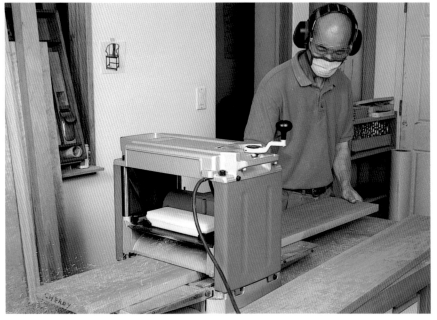

Plane to thickness. A small bench-top thickness planer works well for bringing stock down to the correct thickness quickly and evenly. The high-speed cutterhead leaves a fine surface which only needs light sanding or minimal hand planing.

SELECTING and preparing your material is an essential step before cutting any type of joint. With good stock, your joints will come together flawlessly. Miss this important step and you will compound your difficulties later on. Once your joints are cut, it's equally important to know how to glue-up your work, which involves choosing and spreading glue effectively and employing good clamping and assembly techniques. This section will help steer you in the right direction so your joints come together perfectly every time.

Preparing Your Material

Once you have a clear plan for your project, the first step is to cut all the parts to the right thickness, width, and length. Accurate milling at this stage will pay dividends later when it comes time to put your joints together, because any discrepancies now will only multiply later in the building process. First, I recommend that you avoid pre-milled material, and use roughsawn stock whenever possible—especially for large projects. Boards already milled to thickness at the store aren't stored properly and are often warped, with curved edges and bowed or cupped surfaces, and frequently come with dents or imperfect edges. If you have commercially-milled boards,

please save them for small projects like boxes and the like, so you can cut around the defects. Buy rough stock for your furniture.

Jointing, Planing, Ripping, and Crosscutting

The jointer, thickness planer, and table saw all play a vital role in bringing your work to proper dimension. The following machining sequences will ensure you mill your stock flat, straight, square, and to the correct size.

Face-jointing your lumber is essential if you want to make joints that fit well and build furniture that's flat and square. Before jointing, sight along the board, looking for cup or bow on its face. Then place the cupped or bowed face down on the jointer and take a series of light cuts—about $1/32$ inch—until that side is flat.

With one face flat, run the board flat-side down through the thickness planer, making successive passes until you reach the desired thickness. (See photo, above.) Orient the stock so you plane with the grain to avoid tearout. Be sure to take an even amount of wood from both sides of the board, which means flipping the board over and end-to-end after each pass to orient the grain in the correct direction. This technique reduces the chance of further warping.

After planing, go back to the jointer and joint one edge straight. Keep the face of the board snug to the fence, which keeps the jointed edge stay square. When jointing edges, you can take off a little more than when face-

Check your edges. Accurate right angles are important for joinery. Be sure to use a reliable square to check edges rather than rely solely on your machines' fences.

Smoothing Stock

When milling stock, it's important to understand that, while machines are powerhouses for quickly and effortlessly turning rough stock into flat, dimensioned boards, all power tools leave some form of cutting or machine marks on the surface of your work. In some cases, you'll even get burning. In order to build fine furniture, hand planing or fine sanding is the next step you should undertake before cutting your joints. It's a mistake to leave this step until after cutting the joints, or even after assembly. Smoothing stock after joints are cut risks removing critical material at the joint line, and results in poor-fitting joints. And trying to smooth an assembled piece is next to impossible, since you can't effectively get inside corners and other hard-to-reach areas.

Smoothing with a plane is the surest way to remove mill marks, and done correctly, it leaves surfaces truly flat—an important consideration for joinery work. Make sure your plane iron is sharp, and set it for a light cut. Plane in full passes, slightly overlapping your strokes with each pass to minimize any track marks left by the two corners of the blade. Light sanding with 220- or 320-grit paper after the piece is assembled usually takes care of any slight blemishes, and readies the piece for a coat of finish.

Sanding is another option for removing machine marks, but you must be careful not to round over your carefully prepared surfaces and edges. Be sure to use fresh sandpaper and remember to move up through the grits, starting with 120-grit sandpaper and finishing with 220-grit paper. Sanding by hand with a sanding block is tedious, and is best left for small pieces. If you have access to an industrial wide-belt sander or drum sander, by all means take advantage of one. Power-sanding with a random-orbit sander is an effective small-shop method, but there's a potential danger. A careless sanding approach can leave dips, rounded edges, and scratch marks. The trick is to use a light touch, letting the weight of the sander do all the work so you don't dish the surface.

jointing. A depth-of-cut of about $1/16$ inch is fine. After jointing, check your edges with a square. (See photo, above.) If the square shows that the edges aren't perfectly 90° to the face, readjust your jointer's fence and joint the edges again.

Once you've straightened and squared all your edges, move to the table saw. It's usually best to rip your stock about ¼ inch over final width, especially if you're cutting narrow strips from wider boards. Place the jointed edge against the rip fence for this cut. Go back to the jointer if necessary and re-joint any edges that curve due to tensions released in the ripping process. Finish up on the table saw by ripping to final width, setting the rip fence to the exact dimension you need.

Complete the milling sequence by crosscutting your boards to final length. You can use a miter saw or radial-arm saw for this operation, or use a table saw sled (see page 20). For accuracy, clamp a stop block to your fence when cutting multiple parts to the same length.

Evenly does it. A thin, consistent coat of glue is the best way to ensure a good bond. Use small brushes and sticks—bamboo skewers are excellent—to apply the glue onto broad surfaces and into recesses.

Assembling Joints

Successful joinery depends in large part on a successful glue-up, in which parts go together smoothly and without fuss. Using the right glue and applying it correctly is part of the battle. Another element is making sure you have the right clamps and accessories, and you use them in the correct manner to apply the pressure exactly where it's needed.

Choosing and Applying Glue

Do you need to glue all your woodworking joints? It depends. In furniture construction, many joints will hold together wonderfully by themselves without any glue. But as time passes, wood moves in response to temperature and moisture changes. In addition, many stresses are placed upon furniture during daily use, such as when we repeatedly drag a chair across the floor. Eventually the joints will start to loosen under such conditions. A badly loosened joint is unsafe, but even slight changes can result in joints that squeak uncomfortably.

Some joints, such as certain types of lap joints, do better with the use of nails, screws, pins, or wedges in addition to being glued. Knock-down joints—which are meant to come apart when needed—can be held tightly without glue with the appropriate reinforcing hardware, such as bolts and nuts, or even wooden wedges. Other joints that have no mechanical connection, like biscuits, dowels, and unpegged mortise-and-tenon joints, will need glue for a lasting connection. Dovetails have a wedging effect that helps hold the joint together, but usually in only one plane. Glue keeps the joint tight in the opposite plane. And if your design calls for hidden joints, where you don't want to see reinforcements like nails or pins, you'll need glue here, too.

Today, there's a wide variety of glues for woodworking, and all of them will do fine for holding your joints together soundly. More important are a glue's working characteristics. For almost all of my furniture making, I find that white or yellow glues are the best choice. They're easy to apply, have a relatively long open time (the time you have to get the joints closed once you've spread the glue), clean up easily with water, and dry in a couple hours. Sometimes I add a few drops of water to thin white or yellow glue to give it a little more working time. This makes the glue easier to apply and lets me assemble parts at a more leisurely pace. For outdoor projects that are subject to severe moisture, or for some of the oilier tropical woods, you can use epoxy, plastic-resin, or a polyurethane glue. Keep in mind these glues are generally fussier to work with, require solvents for clean-up, and cost more than ordinary white or yellow glues.

It's important to make sure your joints are well-coated with glue before you put them together. Generally, it's best to brush a thin coat on both parts. (See photo, above.) Remember, if your joints are cut accurately and fit well, it doesn't take much glue for a good bond. Too much glue can cause parts to crack, especially in blind joints where any excess has no place to escape. And excessive glue results in squeeze-out that creates a gooey mess all over your bench and your work. How much is enough? A good rule of thumb is to look for small glue beads along the joint line once you've clamped the joint. When applying glue, I often use narrow sticks, such as bamboo skewers, which you can find at your local grocery store. For deep recesses, such as mortises and other holes, I use a small brush to put an even coat on the wood.

Clamps

THERE ARE many kinds of clamps available for woodworking, and you should stock up on some of the basic ones for general furnituremaking. The photo shows some of my favorites that get frequent use in my shop.

Pipe or bar clamps are some of the most useful, and work well for pulling together flat work such as panels and case parts. Handscrews can be angled to hold angled work, and their wooden jaws can be modified if necessary for special situations. Keep several quick-action clamps on hand; they're great for small clamping jobs, especially across joints such as a mortise-and-tenon. Spring clamps are light duty, but they're handy for quickly grasping parts and often lend a much-needed third hand. Large and small C-clamps, in sizes from 1 inch to 6 inches or more, are a standard in my shop, and get many uses from securing jigs and fixtures to gluing all sorts of small joints with great pressure. I always have one or two band or web clamps kicking around for complex assemblies. The flexible bands wrap around uneven work, making these clamps great for odd assemblies or hard-to-reach areas, such as when gluing together the four corners of a box at the same time. Last, don't overlook some very simple devices that can be used for clamping, such as tape, rubber bands, string—even bungee cords can be used to pull parts together effectively.

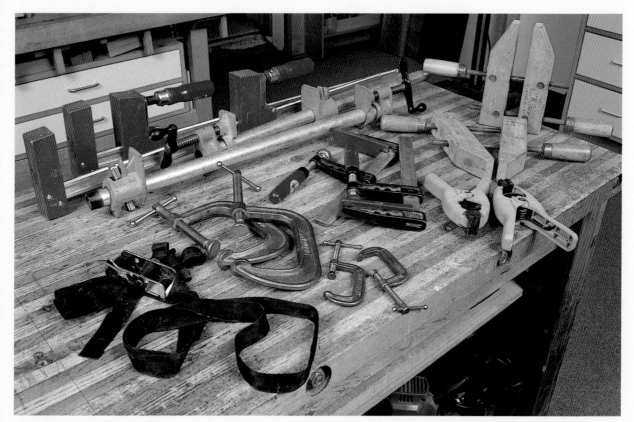

Clamp collection. You'll need a variety of clamps for pulling together different joints, including a selection of pipe or bar clamps, a few wooden handscrews, several quick-action clamps, spring clamps, large and small C-clamps, and one or two band clamps.

Assembly Aids and Techniques

There are many good approaches to assembling your joints and your furniture, and the right clamping technique plays a major role. But other considerations can be just as important, such as practicing the assembly procedure before committing to the real thing as well deciding now what type of finish you'll be using.

Your first consideration should be whether or not to prefinish the parts before assembling them into a whole. Prefinishing is an excellent way to avoid finishing problems, since you can control the finishing process much more easily by working on flat surfaces. Film-type finishes, such as shellac, varnish, or lacquer, can be problematic because they have a tendency build up in corners and other hard-to-reach areas, leaving an uneven tone to the work. Wipe-on penetrating finishes, such as oil and wax, are easy enough to apply after assembly. If you decide to prefinish, make sure you cover any joint areas with masking tape so glue will grab in the right places.

One of the golden rules of assembly is to always pre-assemble, or dry-fit, the parts. This means assembling the entire piece without glue. Once you've cut the joints, dry-fitting lets you rehearse the entire assembly procedure so you can look for potential problems. Now is the time to double-check everything, looking to see that all the parts are cut correctly, nothing is missing, joints fit tight, and the public sides of the wood are facing in the right direction. A dry run will also reveal the correct assembly sequence. For example, you might discover a

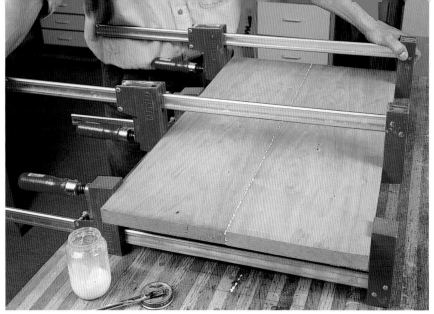

Over and under. Bar clamps are great for gluing together panels and other flat work. Align the clamp screws over the thickness of the work to direct the pressure into the center of the joint, and alternate the clamps over and under to distribute the pressure evenly.

major assembly should be broken down into sub-assemblies, or that parts have to go together in a particular order. After practicing a dry assembly, you can relax a little more during the real thing, which lets you enjoy the assembly process and helps bring good results.

When assembling furniture, clamps not only pull your joints together, but they can become extra helping hands. This is why it's important to choose the right clamps and the right clamping procedure for a specific glue-up. Please remember that you don't need a lot of pressure. Use just enough force so that parts come together and the joint line is tight and without gaps. Excessive clamping will compress the wood or damage a joint, either changing its shape, breaking the work, or sometimes driving too much glue away from the joint line, which results in a starved joint. The following clamping examples will help you decide how to best bring your joints together successfully.

CLAMPING EVENLY

Whenever you apply clamps, be sure to align them correctly on the work. This means centering the pressure from the clamps over the center of the work. For example, when gluing up an edge joint, you should alternate the clamps on the top and bottom to help distribute pressure more evenly, which prevents twisting the panel. Also, be sure to align the centers of the clamps' screws over the thickness of the work, as shown in the photo, above.

FIG. 14

BOWED CAUL

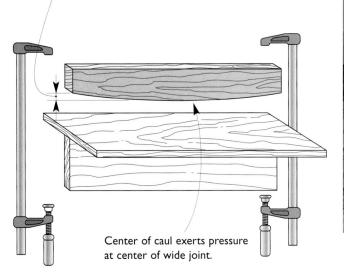

Saw curve in caul by roughly ⅛ in. at each end.

Center of caul exerts pressure at center of wide joint.

Block it out. Small scrap blocks placed over the joint help distribute pressure more evenly and also eliminate the tendency for a clamp to mar the work.

CLAMPING WIDE STUFF

There are many times when it can be difficult to get the clamp pressure where you need it on large workpiece. Once solution is to equip yourself with deep-throat clamps, which can span bigger distances and place force where it's needed. But these clamps are expensive, and you won't find them in most small shops. When you're faced with a wide joint where standard clamps can't reach, a good solution is to use a bowed clamping caul to help distribute the pressure, as shown in the drawing above.

You can make cauls from any type of wood, jointing and milling the edges straight, then introducing a slight curve on one edge with a hand plane or on the bandsaw. By placing the caul over the center of the joint, you can clamp at the ends and effectively bring pressure to bear in the middle.

USING BLOCKS AND PADS

Clamping blocks help distribute pressure, and clamping pads protect the work. Sometimes one block can be used for both, as shown in the top photo, right. Build your blocks from scrap stock, and make sure they have smooth faces where they contact the work to avoid blemishes.

USING TAPE TO PULL PARTS TOGETHER

Don't overlook the power of regular masking tape for clamping power. Tape is a great way to apply pressure when you can't find any other way to access a joint. A good example is when gluing up miters, especially when there are multiple joints to pull together at once, such as when making small boxes or multi-sided cylinders. Start by butting the parts together and applying tape across the joint lines. (See left photos, opposite page.) Carefully flip the assembly over and spread the glue. Finish up by rolling the assembly together, and applying more tape on the outside of the piece.

GLUING ANGLED JOINTS

Many angled joints can be tricky to glue up, since the clamps have a nasty tendency to slip at the worst-possible moment. To overcome this, make a set of scrap blocks with angles cut in them, and clamp these to the individual workpieces. Apply the glue, and assemble the joint by bridging clamps over adjoining blocks, as shown in the middle right photo, opposite page

TAPPING JOINTS HOME

Most joints will need some persuasion before they can be fully clamped together. And interlocking joints, such as through- and half-blind dovetails with their wedged-shaped pins and tails, only need to be coaxed together. No clamps are necessary if you can bring the joint together tightly before the glue starts to set. The trick is to use a hefty block and a sturdy hammer or mallet to bring the joints together. (See bottom photo, below.) Make sure the block is big enough to span the entire width of the joint, and hit the block squarely with the hammer to bring the joints together square and tight.

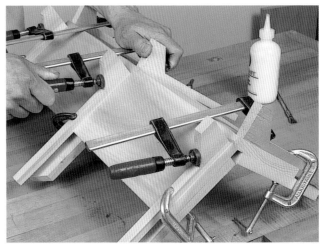

Angled blocks. You can pull tricky stuff, such as miter joints, together with ease by clamping across adjacent blocks secured to adjoining workpieces. Cut the blocks on the bandsaw, making sure opposing faces are 90° to each other.

Tape it tight. Masking tape makes a very effective clamp. Start by stretching the tape over the joint lines (top), and then turn the work over and apply glue (middle above). Finish up by rolling the parts together and applying more tape on the outside (above).

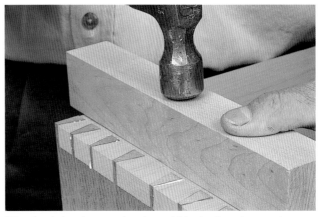

Tap it tight. A stout hardwood block placed over the joint line brings dovetails together without clamps.

Woodworking Joints

THERE ARE eleven categories of joints listed in this book—enough for several homes worth of furniture. In general, you'll find the joints are listed from simple to more complex. For example, the first section on butt joints describes what isn't really a woodworking joint at all, but merely a convenient way to connect two or more flat surfaces. Of course, you'll discover all the common joints used on a daily basis by woodworkers everywhere, such as rabbets and dadoes. More involved joints, such as

dovetails or mortise-and-tenons, are also included. All told, the joints in this book cover practically every construction application you'll ever need to build fine furniture, from panel-making and framework to building cabinets, constructing boxes and drawers, and making chairs and tables.

Choosing the right joint for a particular woodworking project depends on many factors. Do you need a quick solution and a joint that's relatively easy to construct? Or are you looking for a high-end application and a joint

that shows your craftsmanship? Is the piece you're building going to be subjected to a lot of stress (chairs are a good example), warranting a stronger joint? Do you want to use the joint as a part of a design element? Or perhaps you may want to challenge yourself by tackling a more complex joint, or one that's new to you.

To answer these questions, start by looking for a joint that fits your needs. Then check that the joint you want to make can be done on one of your existing machines. You may find that you'll want to acquire a new power tool, or build a jig or two to assist in the joint's construction. The choice is yours, and the information on the following pages will help you decide the right course.

Once you settled on a particular type of joint and its specific construction methodology, I recommend that you first practice on some scraps in order to understand how the joint goes together. Practicing in this manner will also help you to fine-tune your machines to make sure they are set up precisely, and will allow you to test any necessary jigs and fixtures you make. You might even consider building scaled or full-size mock-ups of the furniture you want to build, especially if you're not familiar with a certain type of joint or if you're building a new piece of furniture. Once you're satisfied that the technique you've chosen will work smoothly, go ahead and cut the real thing. With practice, your fine furniture will reflect your new-found joint-cutting skills.

FIG. I

BUTT JOINTS

Edge-to-Edge

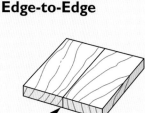

Edges meet square.

Edge-to-Face

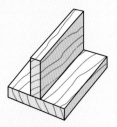

VARIATION

Flush

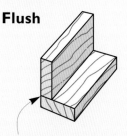

Edge flush with face.

Mitered Edge to Mitered Edge

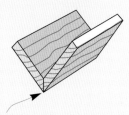

Edges meet at less than 90°; typically 45°.

Butt Joints

The simplest way to join wood, a butt joint is a common feature in all types of furnituremaking and requires simple tools and procedures. This is not an actual joint, but consists of two flat surfaces that are glued together. Butt joints are easy to make and fairly strong. Good uses are for building large panels from individual boards, such as when making tabletops, cabinet sides, or drawer bottoms. If you choose and arrange the grain of the wood carefully, you can make the joint line virtually disappear. Or you can sandwich a different-colored wood between parts as a design element.

The most important feature of a butt joint is that the two mating pieces join long-grain to long-grain. This grain orientation ensures that the glue joint will be sound and the joint will be strong. After you've prepared the material you won't need to do any special cutting, routing, or drilling. Just apply glue to the joint area and clamp.

The main challenge when making a butt joint is to prepare the surfaces perfectly straight, flat, and square, and to align the workpieces carefully during glue-up. Another important aspect is to try to match the wood grain and color as best you can so that the glue line becomes invisible.

Edge-to-Edge

An edge-to-edge joint is probably the most basic type of woodworking joint, and it's easy to construct. It's a good choice when you need to make a wide panel from several narrow boards, a technique often seen in frame-and-panel construction. For a successful glue bond, prepare your mating edges

FIG. 2

Edge-to-Edge

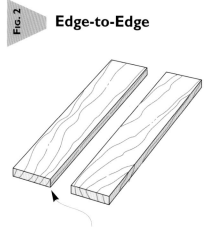

Flat, straight, and square edge

so they're flat, straight, and square. The best way to do this is to joint the edges on a jointer. However, you can also use a sawn edge if the edge is straight and you use a quality saw blade. (For more on saw blades, see page 10.) Don't sand an edge; sanding rounds the edge slightly and weakens the joint. With properly prepared edges, brushed with glue and clamped until the glue dries, this is a strong joint that holds up well for many furniture applications.

Edge-to-Face

Similar to an edge-to-edge joint, an edge-to-face joint requires carefully prepared edges and faces that are flat and smooth. When the joint is assembled it becomes a very stiff structural element, due to the fact that the parts are jointed at right angles to each other. The joint is useful for many furniture applications, and is especially handy for attaching dividers or partitions in casework.

Use the same jointing method as you would an edge-to-edge joint to prepare the edge on one of the parts—either by jointing its edge or ripping it

FIG. 3

Edge-to-Face

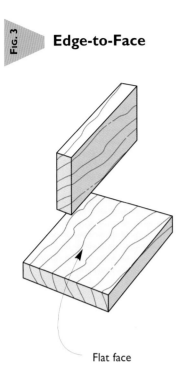

Flat face

with a good saw blade. A joining face that's been thicknessed in a thickness planer is sufficiently flat and ready for gluing and clamping. One important consideration is that an edge-to-face joint is often subject to stress, especially when joining wide parts, such as a divider to a case part in a cabinet. When the joint will be subjected to severe stress, it's best to reinforce the parts with glue blocks. (See Strengthening Butt Joints with Glue Blocks, right.)

A common problem with edge-to-face joints is clamping wide parts. Often, you don't have a clamp deep enough to place pressure in the center of a wide panel. When you run into this situation, you can use a curved beam, or caul, to effectively clamp the area. (See Clamping Wide Joints, page 40.)

Strengthening Butt Joints with Glue Blocks

LONG-GRAIN to long-grain butt joints are incredibly strong, but where a butt joint connects at 90° instead of edge-to-edge, it's often wise to reinforce the connection with glue blocks. When a joint falls in the middle of the work, the simplest method is to use rub blocks on either side of the joint, spreading glue on each block and then rubbing it into the corner of the joint. Be sure to cut the block to exactly 90°, and orient the grain of the block with the grain of the joint. Once you've spread the glue, simply press the block into position. No clamping is necessary. (See photo, below.)

For butt joints at corners, you can strengthen the joint with corner blocks made from soid wood. Make the blocks by cutting them to size on the table saw using a sled equipped with a 45° fence. (See Table Saw Sleds, page 20.) Make sure to cut the blocks to exactly 90°, and then slope the long edge to 45°. (See top photo, right.) Since the edges of the blocks are mostly end grain, you'll need to secure the blocks with screws as well as glue. First countersink holes through each block for wood screws, then glue and screw the block into the corner of the joint. (See middle photo, right.)

The same type of corner block used for butt joints at corners can be used with rail joints, such as where a seat frame joins at the corners. Since the rails butt to each other on end or on edge, the wood grain direction is perpendicular and the glue joint has very little strength. Blocks stiffen the connection. Use the same table saw sled method for cutting the blocks to size on the table saw, then apply glue to the block and secure it to the frame by driving screws through the block and into the adjoining frame members. (See bottom photo, right.)

Rub it in. Triangular rub blocks stiffen the joint, and are easy to install. Use plenty of glue, and simply push them into the corners by hand.

Corner cuts. Use a cut-off sled equipped with a 45° fence to make corner blocks. Cut a 45° miter on one edge, then flip the stock over to miter the adjacent edge.

Screw and glue. Countersink for screws, spread glue on the block, and install it into the corners of the joint.

Rail block. The same block can be used on rail joints to stiffen what is usually an end-grain connection.

Mitered Edge to Mitered Edge

This joint is good for making small or large hollow boxes and posts, such as square pedestals and table columns. Mitered butt joints present a challenge to prepare, and often require special assembly techniques. (For more on assembling miters, see Assembling Joints, page 37.) Since this is a long-grain to long-grain joint, no special reinforcement is necessary, but cutting smooth and accurate miters is all-important. The smoother and flatter the miter, the stronger the joint. Use the table saw to cut the miters.

On the table saw. The table saw is the machine to use for this joint, and you can do the job in two ways. The first approach is to tilt the saw blade to the desired angle, then push the stock past the blade by laying it flat on the saw table and against the rip fence. (See photo, below.) If your joinery involves cutting miters on both edges

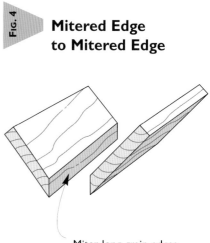
Fig. 4

Mitered Edge to Mitered Edge

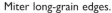

Miter long-grain edges.

of a board, be sure the tip of the first miter doesn't creep under the fence and bind when cutting the second miter. If your fence has a small gap at the table, you can clamp a scrap of plywood to the fence to close the gap.

The second method of cutting a long-grain miter is keep the blade at 90° to the table, which is often more reliable, especially on lighter-duty table saws. This procedure works best on smaller stock. Instead of tilting the

Ripping miters. Bevel the blade 45°, keeping the stock tight against the fence and firmly on the table as you push it through the blade.

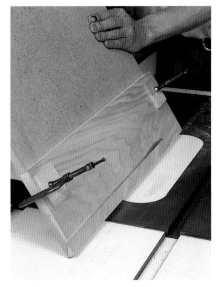

Blade stays 90°. With the jig's fence adjusted to the desired miter angle, clamp the stock with its lower edge parallel with the saw table and push the entire assembly through the blade.

blade, angle the workpiece by clamping it to an adjustable angled fence set to the desired miter angle. (See page 22 for more on the Adjustable Angled Fence Jig.) Once the stock is clamped in place, you can push the assembly past the blade for an accurate miter cut. (See photo, above.)

FIG. 1 ◀ **TONGUE-AND-GROOVE JOINTS**

Edge-to-Edge

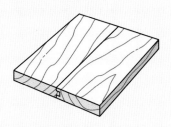

Dovetailed Edge-to-Edge

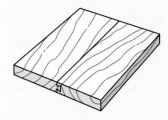

VARIATIONS

Beveled

Cut bevel on both edges.

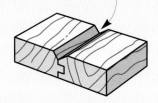

End-Mitered

Pieces meet at 45°.

Bevel and Bead

Cut bevel on tongue board.

Cut bevel and bead on groove board.

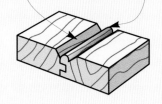

Tongue-and-Groove Joints

The tongue-and-groove is an easy joint to master, and is used widely in furniture and architectural millwork. As figure 1 shows, the basic joint consists of one board with a tongue formed on its edge, which fits into a groove cut in an adjoining board. The joint provides a lot of glue surface and is easy to line up when assembling, especially with long parts. Choose this joint when you want to make large, solid-wood panels from narrow boards. The best example is when making a solid-wood back for a cabinet. By joining a series of tongue-and-groove boards, you can create a wide panel that will allow for wood movement, since each board can move independently. Another plus is that even if the panel shrinks or the glue joint fails, the tongue between individual boards conceals any gaps. Thus, the panel remains closed visually.

Good proportions are key to a strong tongue-and-groove joint. A basic rule of thumb is to make the tongue and its corresponding groove roughly one-third the width of the stock you're working with, and to keep the tongue square. For example, when working with ¾-inch-thick stock, a ¼- by ¼-inch tongue (and its corresponding groove) will maintain the correct proportions and ensure a strong joint. Making the tongue longer or the groove deeper can result in the tongue snapping off or a crack developing above or below the groove.

You can cut either the tongue or the groove first, but it's important to cut the second part in small increments until it fits snugly in the first part. As you fit the tongue or groove, be careful not to make the joint too tight, or it will be difficult to assemble. A sliding fit between the parts is the goal. You can apply glue to this joint, but in many cases no glue is necessary, since the parts lock mechanically. In frame-and-panel construction, a dry joint is especially useful where wood movement is a concern, such as in a series of solid-wood boards for a cabinet back. Here, you can assemble the joint without glue, which allows individual boards to move independently while still maintaining the structural integrity of the joint itself.

One trick to keep in mind with all tongue-and-groove joints is to allow for extra material when dimensioning the part that receives the tongue. This way, both show surfaces will display equal widths when the joint is assembled.

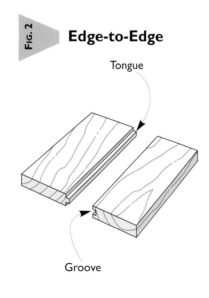

FIG. 2 **Edge-to-Edge**

Tongue

Groove

Edge-to-Edge

The most common tongue-and-groove joint is where two long-grain edges meet, such as in a row of paneling or a series of boards joined edge-to-edge for, say, the back of a cabinet or a floor. Once you master the basic joint, you can add interesting effects by cutting decorative profiles along the edges of the boards where the joint comes together, as shown in figure 1. The basic joint can be cut with the table saw or the router table.

On the table saw. Start by cutting the tongue. You can use a dado cutter, but if it's a small job it's often more convenient to avoid the setup hassle and simply use a standard saw blade. Set the desired height of the saw blade, and with the stock held vertically, adjust the rip fence so the blade cuts about ⅛ inch into the outside face of the board. Make a pass on one face, then position the opposite face against the fence and repeat the cut. Now move the fence closer to the blade and make repeated passes on each face of the stock until you've cut the desired tongue width. (See photo, below.)

Once the tongue has been cut, transfer the tongue width to the adjoining board and, without changing

Tongue cut. Mill the tongue first, using a standard saw blade and cutting on both sides of the stock.

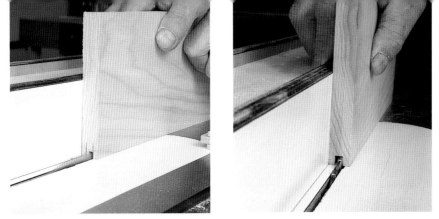

Groove the same way. Without changing the blade height, adjust the fence to cut to your layout lines and rip one side of the groove (left). Then flip the board end-for-end and finish the opposite side (right).

the height of the blade, set the fence to cut just inside the layout lines. Make a cut, then flip the board end-for-end and position the opposite face against the rip fence to make the second cut. Just as you cut the tongue, this technique automatically centers the groove in the board so the joint will come together flush. (See photos, above.) Test the fit of the tongue to the groove, and if it's too tight, move the fence closer to the blade and repeat the cutting procedure until the joint fits easily and without sloppiness. Keep in mind that for each movement of the fence, the amount cut from the tongue will double, making it easy to end up with a loose joint.

On the router table. You have two options for making a standard tongue-and-groove joint. The first method is to use a straight bit, and here it's best to start by cutting the groove. Lay out the groove so it's centered on your stock. Then set the height of the bit and adjust the router fence so the bit is centered over the stock. (You may want to make a test cut on some scrap to get the setup just right.) Once the setup work is done, plough the groove by standing the stock vertically against the fence and pushing it over the bit. (See bottom photo, left.) After the first pass, place the opposite face against the fence and make a second cut to precisely center the groove on the stock.

One disadvantage to using a straight bit is that chips can jam inside the groove. To prevent this, try making a series of shallow cuts, raising the bit with each pass until you reach the desired depth.

To rout the tongue, first lay it out using the previously cut groove. Leave the bit height as is, and adjust the fence so the bit cuts on the inside face of the stock. Make a pass on one face, then rout the opposite face to produce a centered tongue. (See bottom photo, right.) As before, you can keep adjusting the fence in small increments and making repeated passes on both sides of the stock to get a perfect fit between the tongue and the groove.

An alternative method on the router table is to use a slot cutter instead of a straight bit. As before, you'll want to start by cutting the groove first. Here, the advantage of a slot cutter is that chips won't jam inside the groove as you rout. Begin by centering the height of the cutter on the stock's thickness, and adjust the fence for the desired depth of cut. Then place the stock flat on the table and push it past the bit. (See top center photo, opposite page.) One note: If the bit you're using is smaller than the desired width of the groove (when using either a straight bit or a slot cutter), simply keep adjusting the fence (when using a straight bit) or adjust the height of the cutter (when using a slot cutter) and make two or more passes until you've cut the full width of the groove. Another appproach with a slot cutter is to adjust the cutter slightly off center, then rout the groove in two passes by referencing both sides of the stock against the fence. This prevents you from having to adjust the

Vertical routing. Center a straight bit on the stock's thickness, and rout the groove by running the board vertically against the fence.

The tongue is next. Leave the bit height as is, and re-adjust the fence to mill the tongue, taking a pass on each side of the stock until the tongue fits easily into the groove.

cutter height with each pass, and can save time if you're routing a lot of stock.

Routing the tongue is straightforward: Leave the fence setting alone, and lay out the tongue using the previously cut groove. Now adjust the slot cutter height so the cutter aligns with the uppermost layout line with the stock held flat on the table. You may want to make a few test cuts on scrap to check the cutter height. Rout the tongue in two passes by positioning each face of the stock flat on the table with each pass. (See photo, far right.)

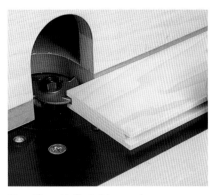

Routing it flat. Use a slot cutter to rout the groove by pushing the stock flat on the table. Flip over the board and make a cut from the other face to widen and automatically center the groove.

Bit and fence remain. Leave the fence setting as is and use the same bit to rout the tongue. Adjust the bit height to cut on the upper face of the board, then make a pass on each face to rout the tongue.

Beads and Bevels Add Flair

TO ADD VISUAL interest to a standard tongue-and-groove, you can create bevels or beads at the edges of the stock where the joints meet. This can be used as a design detail in cabinet panel work. (See fig. 1, page 46.) Once you've cut the tongue and the groove, chamfer both parts by tilting the saw blade on the table saw to 45° or to any other desired angle. Then run both

the grooved board and the board with the tongue past the angled blade. Be sure to adjust the fence for each cut so the chamfers are of consistent width on both parts. (See left photo, below.)

To make a beaded tongue-and-groove joint, cut the basic joint first and then chuck a beading cutter in the router table. Rout a bead on only the groove boards, which

results in a single bead when the joint is brought together. A fancier bead can be made with a beading bit that has a chamfered profile above the bead profile. Rout the bead and chamfer in the groove, and then adjust the cutter height and rout a chamfer above the tongue on the tongue board. (See photo, below.)

Table saw bevels. After you've milled the tongues and grooves, tilt the saw blade to 45° and rip small bevels on all four corners of each board.

Bead with chamfer. After beading the grooved board, use the same cutter to rout small chamfers on the tongue board.

Making Small Fence Adjustments

SNEAKING UP on a fit is an important part of putting joints together successfully. When working on the router table, you can often make a part slightly smaller by adjusting the fence toward or away from the bit in tiny increments, depending on the cut being made. To make this fence adjustment, first strike a pencil line on the far end of the table to mark the fence's current position. Then loosen the clamping arrangement of your fence just a little bit (it should still be snug, not loose), and tap the fence with your hand. (See photo, below.) A small movement of the fence away from the pencil line translates into an even smaller movement at the center of the fence where the bit is, providing great control when sneaking up on the fit. When you have the fence precisely where you want it, be sure to fully tighten the clamps.

Precise taps. A gentle rap with your fist lets you adjust the fence in measurable increments. Lines penciled on the table guide your movement.

FIG. 3 **Dovetail Edge-to-Edge**

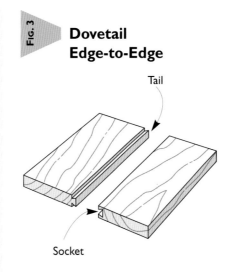

Tail

Socket

Dovetailed Edge-to-Edge

A stronger alternative to the standard tongue-and-groove joint is to dovetail the mating parts. This is an especially useful joint where a strong mechanical connection is needed, such as when joining solid wood boards for the panels on a piece of traditional Chinese furniture, or anywhere you need to make wide panels from smaller boards. Because of the locking nature of the dovetail, the joint doesn't require glue and can be used when you need to take apart the joint later, such as for knockdown furniture. This particular joint is most easily cut on the router table.

You use the same dovetail bit to cut both the socket and the tail. A standard ½-inch bit will cut the joint in stock that's ¾ inch or thicker. However, I often use this joint for very thin (½ inch or less) stock. To do so I modify a standard high-speed steel bit by grinding the top of the bit shorter, reducing its largest diameter to around ¼ inch. (Don't try this technique with carbide-tipped bits.)

Groove first. Rout a narrow groove first with a straight bit, and then mill the dovetail socket using a dovetail bit. This trick reduces stress on the dovetail cutter and produces a cleaner socket.

Tail in two passes. Make sure to keep the bit on the fence side of the workpiece, and rout the dovetail by making a pass on each side of the stock.

On the router table. Cut the dovetail socket first. The first step is to plough a relief groove in your stock, using a small straight bit on the router table or a standard saw blade on the table saw. The idea of this relief cut is to remove as much wood as possible to reduce the amount of cutting the dovetail bit has to do. If you try to rout a full socket with the dovetail bit, wood chips will build up quickly, causing jamming, chatter, and sometimes burning. The result is that you could snap the delicate bit. Center the relief groove in the board that will receive the socket. Be sure the relief groove is narrower than the smallest diameter of the dovetail bit you'll be using, and set the bit or blade height just shy of the finished socket depth. After cutting the straight groove, install a dovetail bit in the router table and roughly center it on the groove by adjusting the fence. Rout the socket in two passes, making the second pass with the opposite face against the fence to automatically center the socket on the stock. (See top photo, opposite page.)

Without changing the height of the dovetail bit, cut the tail next. Fitting a dovetailed tongue-and-groove joint is a hit-or-miss affair. If the joint is too tight, it will be impossible to assemble. Too loose, and there will be very little strength to hold parts together. As with most joint-making operations, it's vital to sneak up on the fit. In this case you'll want to rout the tail in stages, adjusting the fence and taking deeper and deeper cuts until the tail just slides into the dovetail socket.

Adjust the fence so the bit will cut on the inside face of the stock. This setup is important for safety: If the bit is set to cut the outside face, it will grab and throw the workpiece, possibly ruining the cut. Make a few test cuts in scrap to check your setup, then rout the dovetail in two steps by passing each face of the stock past the spinning bit. (See middle photo, opposite page.)

FIG. 4

End-Mitered

Saw protruding tongue flush after assembly.

End-Mitered

The end-mitered joint is often used for framework, frequently for door frames or wherever you need a frame with mitered corners. The joint is very common in Chinese furniture, and is typically glued, since it hasn't much locking or mechanical strength on its own. The joint can be cut on the table saw or on the router table with the aid of a few jigs.

On the table saw. You'll cut the groove first, then fit the tongue to the groove. Begin by using the table saw sled with a 45° fence attached (see page 20) to cut miters on the ends of the stock. Once the miters are cut, you'll need the tenoning jig (see page 23) onto which you clamp two 45° fences. You can cut the groove with a single pass using a dado blade, or you can make multiple passes using a standard saw blade, flipping the stock over on the second pass to cut a perfectly centered groove. (See top photo, right.)

Now cut the tongue to fit the groove. Using the same jig setup, clamp the stock to one of the fences

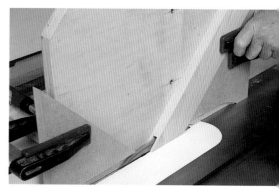

Angled groove. Use the tenoning jig, with two 45° fences clamped to it, to saw the groove. A single saw blade makes the cut if you flip the stock and position it on the opposite fence for a second pass.

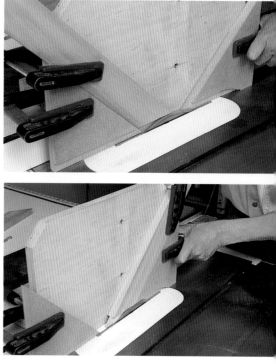

Cheek two-step. Cut the tongue with the same setup, ripping the first cheek by positioning the board on one of the angled fences (top). Rip the opposite cheek with the stock clamped to the opposite fence (above).

Angled block makes it safe. With a slot cutter chucked in the table, cut the groove by running the stock against a zero-clearance fence, backing it up with a block of scrap MDF cut to a 45° angle.

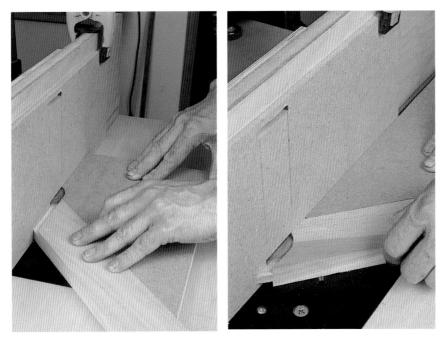

Angled tongue. Use the same block to rout the tongue, making a pass on one side (left) and then reversing the block and flipping the board over for the second pass (right).

and rip the first cheek. Then clamp the stock to the opposite fence and rip the second cheek. (See bottom photos, previous page.)

On the router table. The procedure is similar to that used on the table saw, since you cut the groove first, then the tongue. Install a slot cutter in the router, and clamp a zero-clearance fence (see page 29) to the existing fence to support the workpiece. Make a push block by cutting a scrap of MDF at a 45° angle, and use the block to guide the work past the bit. (See photo, left.) It's a good idea to test your set-up on some scrap first to ensure the bit is centered on the stock before cutting the actual workpiece.

Without changing the depth of cut, rout the tongue in two passes. Raise the height of the bit (test the setup on scrap) and rout the first cheek, again using the angled push block. Then flip the stock over and reverse the push block to cut the second cheek. (See photos, left.)

FIG. I ◄ **SPLINE JOINTS**

Edge-to-Edge

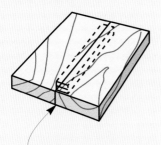

VARIATION

Blind Spline

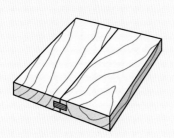

Spline is hidden at ends of joint.

Edge-to-Face

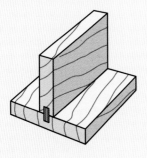

End-to-Face

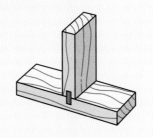

End-to-Edge

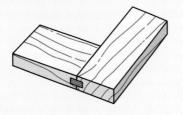

Edge-Mitered

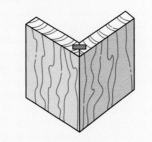

Face-Mitered

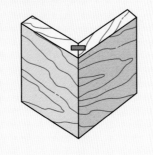

End-Mitered

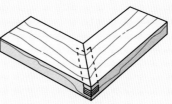

End-Mitered Feather

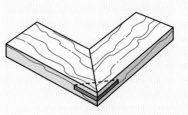

Compound Angle

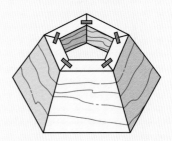

Spline Joints

Spline joints are commonly used in furniture, cabinets, and architectural millwork. You can use spline joints to make a large panel from smaller pieces, but the splines will show at both ends unless you stop them in from the ends. Spline joints are good for solid wood, plywood, and MDF. With this type of joint, the spline itself is the connector between the two workpieces. The joint is easy to make, very strong, and self-aligning during glue-up.

Splines can be made from a variety of materials. (See Choosing and Making Splines, right.) Plan on making the thickness of your splines equal to the width of the grooves so they fit into the grooves easily but without any side-to-side play. Spline width should be slightly less than twice the depth of one groove, or slightly under the total depth of two adjacent grooves. If you make your splines wider than this, you run the risk of not being able to close the joint during glue-up.

Edge-to-Edge

An edge-to-edge spline joint is similar to a tongue-and-groove joint. It's equally strong, and you can use it for similar applications, generally in making wider panels from narrow boards. The table saw, router table, hand-held router, and biscuit joiner can all be used to construct this type of joint.

On the table saw. Adjust the saw blade height to the desired depth of the groove, then hold the stock on edge against the fence to cut the groove. You can use a standard saw blade to make a groove wider than ⅛ inch by making two passes, running each side of the stock against the fence with each pass. Or use a dado blade stacked to the desired width of the groove. Run all your stock with the same setup, then make the splines to fit the grooves.

A variation on the standard edge-to-edge spline joint is a blind spline, where you don't see the spline at the ends of the joint. The trick is to stop the groove about ½ inch inside each end of the stock. You can do this by lowering your stock onto the spinning saw blade, referencing the stock against a mark on the rip fence that indicates the start of the cut. Finish the groove by stopping the cut at a second mark and lifting the work upward and off the blade. This technique takes practice, and must be done safely or you risk having the stock thrown back at you, especially when beginning the cut. An easier and safer method is to use the router table or a handheld router for cutting blind grooves.

Choosing and Making Splines

▶ **YOU CAN USE** plywood or solid wood for splines. Plywood is the strongest because of its cross-grain construction, and you can cut plywood splines without regard for grain direction. But plywood often shows a different color or texture on the end of an exposed joint. When the spline is a visual part of the joint, you're better off choosing solid wood. Here, grain direction is important. When using solid wood, be careful to orient the grain in the same direction and try to match the color and grain of the spline with the work so it will blend in with the finished project.

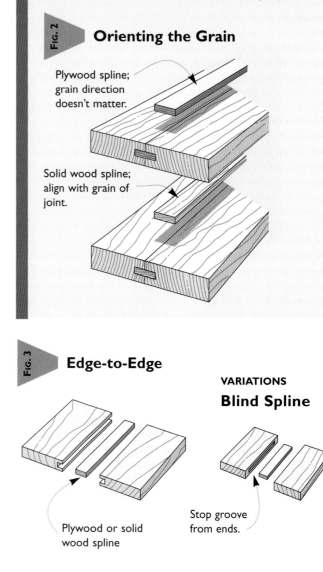

FIG. 2 Orienting the Grain

Plywood spline; grain direction doesn't matter.

Solid wood spline; align with grain of joint.

FIG. 3 Edge-to-Edge

Plywood or solid wood spline

VARIATIONS

Blind Spline

Stop groove from ends.

Stopped cut. Pieces of masking tape indicate where to start and stop the cut for a blind groove.

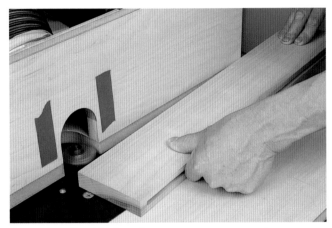

Stopping flat. With a slot cutter, you can use the same blind-cutting technique by laying the stock flat on the table. The cut feels safer since you can more easily pivot the work into the bit.

Curved to fit. Shape the end of the spline to match the curved ends of the slots.

On the router table. There are two ways to cut an edge-to-edge spline joint on the router table. The first is to install a straight bit in the table, adjusting the fence so the bit is centered on the edge of the stock. Then stand the workpiece on edge and run it against fence to cut the slot.

The second method uses a slot cutter, adjusting its height so the bit is centered on the stock's thickness. Set the fence so the slot cutter protrudes to the desired slot depth. Then lay the stock flat on the table and run its edge against the fence to cut the slot. To make a slot wider than the cutting width of your slot cutter, mark the width of the slot on your stock and adjust the cutter to cut to one side of your marks. Then rout the slot in two passes. The first pass will cut a slot to the first mark. Now flip the stock over and make a second cut, which will automatically center the slot.

Both setups mentioned above can be used to cut blind spline joints. With the straight-bit method, apply two strips of tape to the fence to mark the beginning and end of the cut, then lower the stock onto the spinning bit at your first mark. (See top photo, left.) Run the workpiece against the fence until you reach the second mark, and lift the stock up and away from the bit.

When using a slot cutter, use the same method of marking the fence with tape for the beginning and end of the slot, and pivot your stock into the spinning cutter to begin the cut. (See photo, left.) When the stock reaches your second mark, pivot the opposite end away from the fence and cutter to stop the cut. Since the slot cutter will leave a rounded groove at each end, you'll need to round both ends of your spline material to fit. (See bottom photo, left.)

With a hand-held router. An edge-to-edge spline joint is easy to cut with a hand-held router and a straight bit, as long as you find some way to guide the router when routing the slots in your boards. The technique works best with a plunge router. There are two approaches you can take: The first is to clamp your work in the bench vise, then clamp a straightedge to the bench (a straight piece of plywood is a good choice) such that the straightedge is parallel to and the correct distance from the stock. Adjust the bit to cut to the correct depth of the groove, and check that the bit is centered on the stock's thickness. Then guide the router against the straightedge as you cut the groove. You can use the same technique to rout a stopped groove for blind splines, as shown in the top photo, next page.

Plywood fence. Rout a stopped groove by plunging a straight bit into the work, registering the base of the router against a straightedge. Pencil marks let you gauge where to stop the cut.

Edge control. A commercial edge guide controls the router and registers the bit in the center of the stock. Scrap stock taped to the baseplate steadies the router.

The second approach is to use an edge guide fitted to the router to cut the grooves. Clamp the stock in your bench vise with the stock protruding about 1 inch above the bench surface, and adjust the edge guide to bear against the workpiece with the bit centered on the stock. To stabilize the router and keep it from tipping during the cut, secure a scrap block to the baseplate with double-faced (carpet) tape. The block's height should exactly match the amount the workpiece protrudes above the bench. Then rout the groove in one pass, riding the baseplate on the edge of the workpiece while the block rides the benchtop. Again, the same setup can be used to cut stopped grooves for blind splines. (See middle photo, left.)

With a biscuit joiner. Although a biscuit joiner is best used for cutting slots for biscuits, you can also use the tool for cutting grooves for spline joints. Make sure to firmly clamp the stock to your workbench. Then set the depth of cut on your joiner to the desired groove depth. To center the cutter on the edge of the stock, you can either adjust the joiner's fence or remove the fence and insert shims between the workpiece and the bench until the stock is centered on the joiner's cutter. Start the cut by plunging into the stock at one end, then slide the joiner sideways, moving the tool against the cutter's rotation, until you've cut a full-length groove.

FIG. 4 **Edge-to-Face**

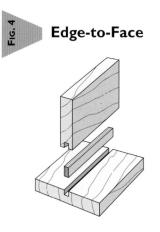

Edge-to-Face

This is a good joint for cabinet framework, or when you need to join the edge of a panel to a wide surface, such as attaching a divider to a cabinet. The glued and assembled joint is strong since it relies on the spline itself as well as the long-grain to long-grain gluing surfaces. Construction is similar to making an edge-to-edge joint, and can be done on the table saw, router table, or with a hand-held router.

On the table saw. Use the same setup as when cutting an edge-to-edge joint (see page 47), adjusting the blade height to the desired depth of the groove and setting the rip fence to center the groove. To cut the groove in the vertical piece, position the stock on edge and run its face against the fence. Without changing the height of the saw blade, reset the fence to mill a groove in the center of the horizontal piece by positioning the work flat on the table.

On the router table. Use a straight bit in the router table to rout the grooves in both vertical horizontal pieces, adjusting the bit height to correspond

FIG. 5

End-to-Face

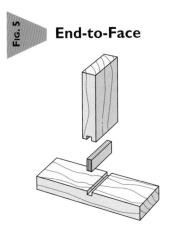

with the desired depth of the groove. Adjust the fence to center the bit on the edge of the work for routing the vertical piece, and use a tall fence when making the cut. (See High/Low Router Table Fence, page 27.) Readjust the fence for routing the groove in the horizontal piece, and push the work over the bit with it flat on the table.

With a hand-held router. You can use an edge guide to rout the groove in the vertical piece, clamping the work on edge in a bench vise and using the same setup as when cutting an edge-to-edge spline joint. (See page 55.) Or you can groove the vertical piece by clamping it in the vise and clamping a straightedge to the benchtop, using the same procedure for cutting an edge-to-edge joint.

To rout the groove in the horizontal piece, clamp the stock to the benchtop, then clamp a straightedge to the stock. The edge of the stock should be parallel to and the correct distance from the edge of the router. Guide the router against the straightedge as you cut the groove.

End-to-Face

An end-to-face spline joint is a good choice when building frames, or when constructing shelves and positioning rails. Generally, this joint is best used with narrow workpieces. The strength of the joint relies on the glued spline itself, since the joined surfaces are end-grain to face-grain. You can use the table saw or the router table to make the joint.

On the table saw. Clamp the vertical piece in the tenoning jig (see page 23) to mill the groove in its end. Set the blade height to the desired groove depth, and adjust the rip fence to center the stock over the blade. Then use the double-runner sled (see page 21) to crosscut the groove in the horizontal piece, adjusting the blade height to account for the thickness of the sled and laying the stock flat on the sled. Use a stop block clamped to the sled's fence to locate the groove correctly on the workpiece.

On the router table. Rout the end groove in the vertical piece with the work standing upright and against a high fence. (See High/Low Router Table Fence, page 27.) Chuck a straight bit in the table, and adjust its height to the depth of the groove. Adjust the fence to center the bit. For workpieces less than 6 inches wide, use a wide piece of scrap behind the work to help steady it as you run both pieces over the bit.

To rout the groove in the horizontal piece, leave the bit height as is, and use the sliding fence (see page 29) to push the work over the bit. Lay the stock flat on the table, and use a stop block clamped to the fence, or mark the stock and gauge the cut by eye.

End-to-Edge

This joint is used extensively in frame construction, particularly with flat frames, such as the stiles and rails for a door or a face frame. Like an end-to-face spline joint, there is very little strength between the adjoining members since one piece consists of end grain. A well-fitted and glued spline is the strongest approach with this type of joint. The joint is a little tricky to make in that one member—the stile—receives a stopped groove. You can make this joint on the table saw or on the router table.

On the table saw. Set the blade height to the desired groove depth. Cut the end-grain slot in the rail first, clamping the workpiece upright in the tenoning jig (see page 23) and adjusting the rip fence so the blade is centered on the work.

To cut the stopped groove in the stile, leave the blade height as it is and remove the tenoning jig, then reset the fence to center the edge of the stock on the blade. Clamp a stop block at the far end of the fence to correspond to the length of the groove in the work. Run the stock on its long edge

FIG. 6

End-to-Edge

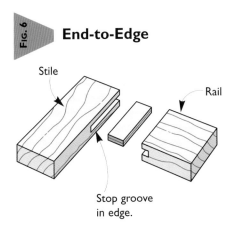

Stile

Rail

Stop groove in edge.

and into the blade, stopping when the work contacts the stop block. You'll have to square up the end of the groove with a chisel since the saw blade will leave a curvature in this area. Keep in mind that a small diameter saw blade will leave less curvature at the end of the cut.

On the router table. Routing the slots on the router table is much easier than using the table saw, especially if you use a straight bit. Set the bit height to the groove depth and use a tall fence (see High/Low Router Table Fence, page 27) to guide the work. Adjust the fence so the bit is centered on the stock's thickness, and rout the groove in the end of the rail by standing the rail vertically. Use a wide scrap block behind the rail as you push it past the bit to steady it and keep it from tipping.

Without changing the bit height or fence setting, rout the stopped groove in the stile. First clamp a stop block to the fence on the far side of the bit, then push the stock on its long edge and into the bit until it contacts the block. The small curve left by the router bit at the end of the slot is easily cleaned up with a few cuts from a chisel.

A second method for routing the slots is to use a slot cutter. Center the cutter on the thickness of the stock and adjust the fence for the correct depth of cut. Rout the end of the rail by laying the stock flat on the table and using a wide piece of scrap behind the work to guide it. Then rout the stile by marking the fence for the stopped cut, or by clamping a stop block the correct distance from the bit. Push the stock flat on the table with its edge against the fence, stopping when the work reaches the mark or the stop block. Since the slot cutter will leave a small curvature at the end of the cut, some chisel work is necessary to square up the cut.

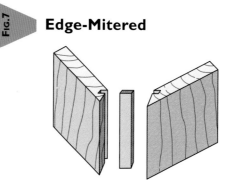

Fig. 7

Edge-Mitered

Edge-Mitered

A splined edge miter is useful when constructing case panels, such as an angled panel for a cabinet, pedestal, or door—even small boxes. While the miters themselves are strong when glued together due to their long-grain surfaces, adding a spline into the joint makes it easier to align the parts during glue-up and adds more strength. Cutting accurate miters is the key to constructing this joint. (For more on cutting accurate miters, see Jigs for Accurate Joints, page 20.) Once you've cut the miters, milling the slot for the spline can be done on the table saw or the router table. For the strongest possible joint, be sure to locate the slots for the spline as close to the root of the miter as possible. (See Locating Splines in Miter Joints, below.)

On the table saw. Once you've accurately cut the miters in the stock, you have a couple options for milling the grooves for the spline. If you're working with large panels, such as case sides, it's best to tilt the saw blade to an angle that's perpendicular to the face of the miter (typically 45° if your

Locating Splines in Miter Joints

WHEN ADDING a spline to a miter joint, it's important to pay attention to the location of the spline itself to maximize its strength. The trick is to cut the slots for the spline at the root of the miters, as shown in the drawing. This technique lets you cut deeper slots (and use a wider spline) without cutting through to the face or outside of the joint.

Fig. 8

Locating the grooves

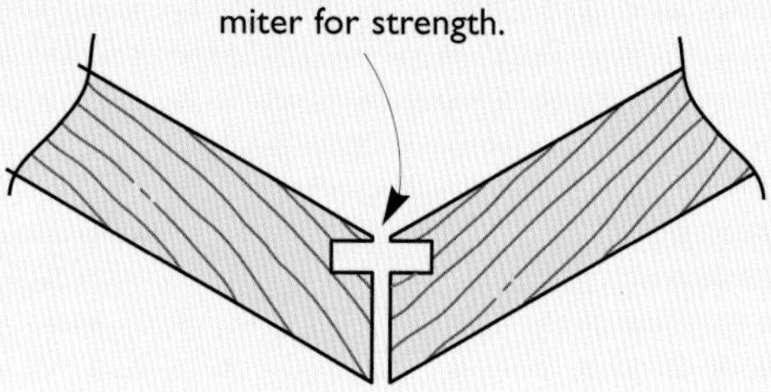

Cut groove at root of miter for strength.

Accurate groove. Clamp the stock parallel with and onto the adjustable angled fence, and then mill a 45° groove with the blade at 90° to the table.

miters are cut at 45°). Lay the work flat on the table, set the rip fence so the saw blade cuts close to the root of the miter, and push the panel over the blade, letting the tip of the opposite miter ride against the rip fence.

For smaller work, such as the sides of a box or small pedestal, it's more accurate to cut the grooves using the adjustable angled fence jig (see page 22). Adjust the height of the saw blade to the desired depth of the groove, then clamp the stock to the jig with its mitered edge flat on the saw table. Set the rip fence so the blade is close to the inside, or root of the miter. (See Locating Splines in Miter Joints, opposite page.) Then slide the jig and the work along the rip fence to cut the groove. (See photo, above.)

On the router table. For short stock, the router table is a good approach when equipped with a slot cutter and the adjustable angled fence. (See page 22.) Start by clamping the base of the jig lightly to the router table. Place the stock on the angled fence with the miter facing up and adjust the angle of the fence until the miter is tight against the router fence, then clamp the angled fence fast. This arrangement will orient the jig's fence at the correct angle. Now adjust the jig's base until the slot cutter is located at the root of the miter. Once you're satisfied with the set-up, fully tighten the clamps and push the stock past the bit, using an even feed speed. The setup is identical to routing a face miter, as shown in the bottom photo on the next page.

Face-Mitered

A face-mitered spline joint is practically identical to an edge miter, except that the orientation of the grain results in miters with end-grain surfaces. Because of this, a spline is necessary and adds tremendous strength to the joint. This is a good joint for the mitered sides of a box or small case, particularly when working with solid wood. Once you've cut the miters (see Jigs for Accurate Joints, page 20), you can cut the joint on the table saw or the router table.

On the table saw. Begin with the saw blade at 90°, and adjust its height to the desired groove depth. Install the adjustable angled fence (see page 22) on the saw's rip fence, adjusting the fence so that the face of the miter on your stock is positioned flat on the saw table when the stock is placed on the fence. Screw or clamp a straight piece of scrap to the angled fence at right angles to the saw blade, and add a few hold-down clamps on top of the scrap piece. Clamp the stock against the scrap, with its miter facing down and against the saw table. Move the rip fence to align the blade to the desired groove location, and run the assembly over the blade. (See top photo, next page.)

On the router table. To cut this joint on the router table you'll use the adjustable angled fence (see page 22) and a slot cutter. Adjust the jig's fence so the stock's miter is flat on the router table fence, then lightly clamp the jig to the router table. Place the stock with its miter facing up on the angled fence, and readjust the fence so the slot cutter is positioned near the root of the miter. Tighten the clamps, then push the stock past the bit using a wide piece of scrap to back up the cut and guide the workpiece. (See bottom photo, next page.)

FIG. 9   **Face-Mitered**

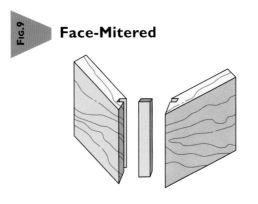

On the table saw. A fence screwed to the jig at a right angle to the saw blade lets you orient the work correctly for cutting a 45° groove in the end of the board. Toggle clamps keep the stock secure and fingers safe.

On the router table. Use a slot cutter and the adjustable-angled jig on the router table to cut the groove. For strength, line up the cutter height with the root of the miter.

End-Mitered

End miters are useful for constructing frames. A big advantage when making these joints is that the machine work on all the parts is the same, making the setup simple and easy. You can construct these joints on the table saw or router table with the help of a few jigs. Start by cutting the miters (see Jigs for Accurate Joints, page 20), then choose the machine of your choice.

On the table saw. Start by cutting the miters on the ends of the stock, using a 45° fence attached to the table saw sled (see page 20). Then use the tenoning jig (see page 23) fitted with two 45° fences, which is the same setup used when cutting a tongue-and-groove end miter, as shown in the photos on page 51. Cut the groove for the spline with a single pass using a dado blade, or make multiple passes using a standard saw blade, flipping the stock over for the second pass and clamping it to the opposite fence to cut a perfectly centered groove. Be sure to make your splines slightly longer than necessary, then glue and assemble the joint. Once the glue has dried, trim the excess spline material flush with the joint with a hand saw or chisel.

On the router table. Routing this joint is safer than using the table saw, since you can work with the stock flat on the table and use a slot cutter, which cleans out the waste while cutting. Start by chucking a slot cutter in the router, and install a zero-clearance fence. Use a scrap block to help guide the work past the bit, cutting a 45° angle on one edge of the block. The setup and technique is identical to cutting an end miter for a tongue-and-groove joint. (See photo, page 52.)

Fig. 10

End-Mitered

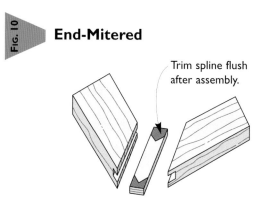

Trim spline flush after assembly.

End-Mitered Feather

Adding a wooden "feather" or spline to an end miter is a great way of strengthening what is essentially a weak end-grain joint. This is a common technique for making all sorts of 45° mitered frames, including picture frames. The feather provides good long-grain gluing surfaces, and can be used as a decorative element in the finished project. You can cut the joint on the table saw or the router table, using the special jig shown in figure 12.

On the table saw. Cut the miters using the table sled, and be sure to mark adjoining miters. Clamp the feather spline jig to the tenoning jig (see page 23). Set the saw blade height to the desired depth of the slot, and clamp two adjoining miters into the jig. Adjust the rip fence to center the blade on the work, then push the jig and the stock through the blade to cut the slots. (See photo, below.)

Once you've slotted all the frame pieces, thickness-plane or rip on the table saw a length of feather stock until it fits snug into the slots. Cut out oversized feathers on the bandsaw or on the table saw, then glue and assemble the miters and install the feathers into the slots with glue. Once the glue has dried, trim the feathers flush to the frame with a hand plane or chisel.

Two jigs together. Clamp the feather spline jig to the tenoning jig, secure adjoining miters into the jig, and then slide the assembly over the blade to cut a slot across the miters.

FIG. 11

End-Mitered Feather

Fit and trim "feather" after assembly.

FIG. 12

Feather Spline Jig

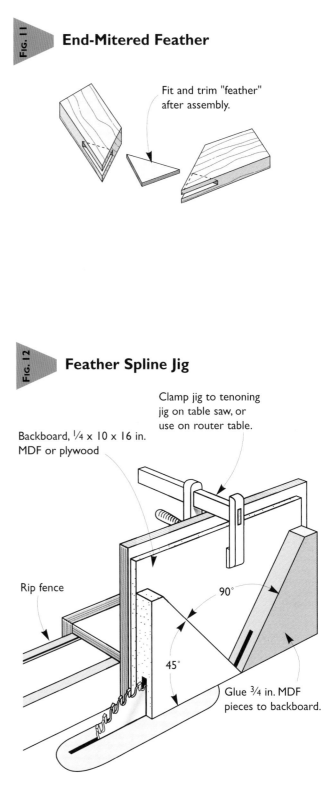

Clamp jig to tenoning jig on table saw, or use on router table.

Backboard, ¼ x 10 x 16 in. MDF or plywood

Rip fence

90°

45°

Glue ¾ in. MDF pieces to backboard.

Routing slots for feathers. Position mating miters in the feather spline jig and use a slot cutter to rout a slot across the joint.

On the router table. Cut the miters using the table saw sled, and then install a slot cutter in the router table. Clamp the feather spline jig (see fig. 12, previous page) against the router fence, and adjust the height of the slot cutter to center it on the thickness of the workpiece. One note: There's a potential disadvantage with this operation, since a thick fence will minimize the total slot depth you can cut in the work, based on the relatively small diameter of most slot cutters. The trick is to use a thinner fence to gain the maximum depth of cut. Once you've set up the cutter and fence, position a pair of miters in the jig, and run the entire assembly past the blade to cut the slot, as shown in the photo, above. Glue and assemble the joint as mentioned under the table saw approach, previous page.

Compound Angle

This is an interesting joint, good for making special cases, boxes, or bases. Compound-angled spline joints must be mitered, and you'll need to calculate the correct miter angles depending on the total number of sides of the box you're building. I find that experimenting on scrap stock is the best way to determine the appropriate angles, one angle for the miters and another angle for the degree that the sides slope. Once you've found the angles on your scrap, record them so you can set up your fences and cutters.

While you can cut the grooves for the splines on the table saw or router table, cutting the miters themselves is best done on the table saw. Use the table saw sled fitted with an angled fence (see page 20). Make the fence to the desired slope angle of the sides, then tilt the saw blade to the miter angle. Begin by cutting one end of each part with the stock held against the fence, as shown in the top left photo, opposite page. Once you've

mitered one end of all the pieces, nail or screw a stop block to the base of the sled and cut the opposite ends to finished length. (See top middle photo, opposite page.)

On the table saw. Use the adjustable angled fence on the table saw's rip fence (see page 22), adjusting the fence to the miter angle. With the saw blade at 90° and set to the desired groove depth, clamp the stock to the angled fence with its miter down on the saw table and run the work over the blade. (See top right photo, opposite page.) Groove both ends of all the parts in this manner, then cut your splines to fit the grooves.

Gluing a compound-angled spline joint can be a challenge. The best approach is to glue up one joint at a

FIG. 13

Compound Angle

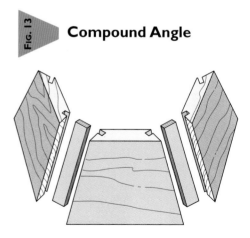

Complex angles made easy. With the saw blade tilted to the miter angle, cut the compound angle by holding the work against an angled fence nailed to the table saw sled.

Precise lengths. Trim the opposite end to length by registering the work against the opposite edge of the fence. A stop block nailed to the base lets you cut multiple parts to the same length.

Grooving odd angles. Once you've cut all the compound angles on the ends of the stock, use the adjustable angled fence to cut the slots for splines. With the blade at 90°, clamp the stock to the jig's fence and push the assembly over the blade.

time, then join individual assemblies after the glue has dried. To make gluing each joint foolproof, make a few clamping blocks from scrap wood to give purchase to your clamps. Clamp the blocks to the work, then clamp across the blocks to pull the joint home. (See photo, right.)

On the router table. Cutting the grooves on the router table is best done with the adjustable angled fence (see page 22) and a slot cutter. Adjust the angle of the fence to the miter angle on the stock, then position the work on the jig's fence with its miter facing up and against the router fence and lightly clamp the jig to the router table. Check that the cutter is positioned at the root of the miter, tighten the clamps, and push the stock past the cutter. The setup is similar to cutting a face miter for a box, as shown in the photo on page 60. Glue and assemble the joint as you would using the table saw method mentioned above.

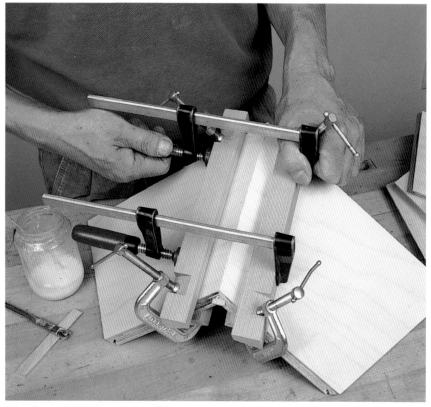

Blocks help pull it tight. Gluing compound-angled joints is a challenge, and is easiest if you assemble one joint at a time. Angled blocks clamped to the work let you position your clamps across and square to the joint line.

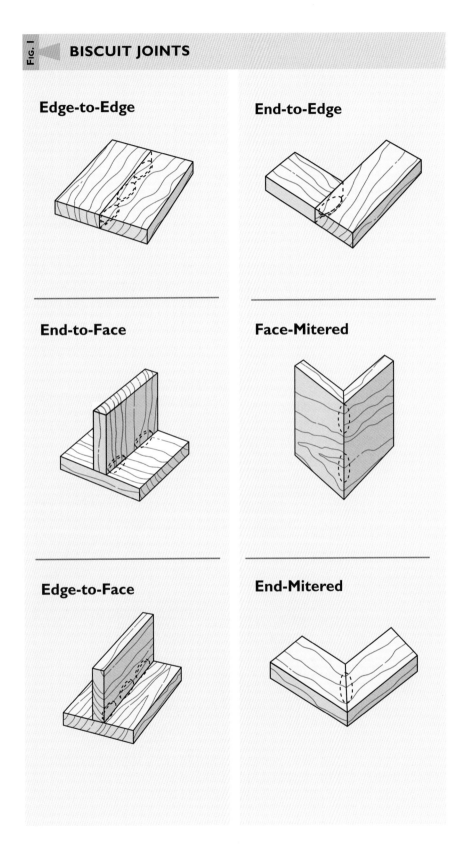

FIG. 1

BISCUIT JOINTS

Edge-to-Edge

End-to-Edge

End-to-Face

Face-Mitered

Edge-to-Face

End-Mitered

Biscuit Joints

The biscuit joint, also called a plate joint, is a relatively new type of joint that's very simple to construct. You cut a series of slots in adjoining pieces with a biscuit joiner, then glue compressed wooden plates, or biscuits, into the slots. The biscuits swell from contact with the moisture in the glue, making a very strong joint. Biscuit joints can be used with solid wood as well as sheet stock such as plywood and MDF, making them suitable for cabinet construction and casework.

Because of the ease of layout, setup, and cutting, biscuit joints can replace spline joints in many cases. One example is when using this type of joint in sheet stock and other large panels, since you can move the biscuit joiner to cut the joint instead of moving the workpiece. And you avoid the awkwardness of having to drill, rout, or saw into the middle of wide stock or narrow edges. A biscuit joiner handles these tasks very well. But biscuits work equally well for smaller projects, such as boxes, small bases, and frames. Another benefit to biscuit joints is their ability to register workpieces easily and accurately. Like a spline joint, mating edges can be lined up precisely during assembly, making glue-up foolproof.

The first step when constructing a biscuit joint is to choose the right size of biscuit, depending on the thickness of the stock you're working with. (See Choosing Biscuits, opposite page.) Once you've decided on the correct size of the biscuits, for most joints you adjust the height of the joiner's fence to align its cutter with the center of your stock. Other joints require no fence at all, registering instead from the base of the joiner itself.

Edge-to-Edge

Commonly used for cabinet construction and casework, an edge-to-edge biscuit joint is a simple butt joint reinforced with biscuits every 8 inches or so. This is a handy joint when making larger panels from smaller boards. The biscuits add strength to an already strong long-grain to long-grain joint, and they also provide a convenient method for aligning the surfaces of adjoining boards.

Start by laying out the slot locations, which is a very simple affair.

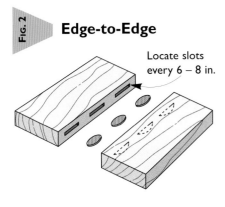

FIG. 2

Edge-to-Edge

Locate slots every 6 – 8 in.

Position the boards edge to edge as they will go together, and strike a line every 6 to 8 inches across the joint for each biscuit. You don't have to be fussy with your layout; the biscuits slots will have enough lengthwise play in them so you can align the joint precisely during glue-up. (See photo, below.) Slot each board with the biscuit joiner, making sure to reference the same face for each board and checking that the appropriate depth of cut is set for the biscuit size you're using.

End-to-Face

Used in cabinetwork and framework, an end-to-face biscuit joint can be used in narrow stock, but typically it's used when joining wide panels at 90° to each other. You can use solid wood or sheet stock. In solid wood, one half of the joint is end grain, so the addition of biscuits is necessary to make a strong connection. Regardless of the type of stock you use, the biscuits themselves are a great aid when it comes to aligning the parts accurately during glue-up.

There are two approaches when cutting the biscuits slots for an end-to-face joint, depending on the specific location of the parts.

Laying out for biscuits. Position the boards edge-to-edge, then strike across the joint line every 6 to 8 inches for biscuit slots.

Choosing Biscuits

There are three essential biscuit sizes for furniture work: #0, #10, and #20. (See photo, page 16.) Some manufacturers make "mini-biscuits" and oversized biscuits, but these require special cutters and often a specialized biscuit joiner as well. To cut the correct slot depth, you adjust a dial or stop on the biscuit joiner to correspond to the size of the biscuit you're using. When making biscuit joints, choose the largest biscuit possible depending on the size of your stock in order to gain maximum strength in the joint.

Biscuit size	Width (in.)	Length (in.)	Slot length (in.)	Minimum stock thickness
0	$5/8$	$1\,7/8$	$2\,3/16$	$3/8$
10	$3/4$	$2\,1/8$	$2\,3/8$	$1/2$
20	$15/16$	$2\,1/4$	$2\,1/2$	$9/16$

FIG. 3

End-to-Face

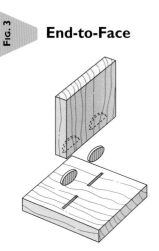

To construct an end-to-face joint where the parts meet flush on a corner, begin by dry-assembling the joint, then striking across it to mark for biscuits. (See middle left photo, below.) Cut the slots in the end of the board with the stock flat on the workbench, aligning the joiner and its fence with your marks. If the base of the joiner extends below the board, prop the panel on top of another piece to lift it off the bench surface. (See photo, below.)

Clamp the second panel on edge in a bench vise, and balance the joiner's fence on the edge of the panel to cut the slots in the face. (See bottom photo, left.) Use a steady hand, making sure the joiner remains square as you plunge into the workpiece.

Joining the end of a panel to the middle of another panel is a common cabinetmaking task, such as when building shelves, partitions, or dividers. The following technique works particularly well for sheet stock that's ¾ inch thick. For thinner or thicker stock, you'll need to either add shims under the workpiece or tape shims to the base of the joiner to center the cutter on the stock's thickness. First lay out where the joint meets on one edge of the face panel. With the face panel laying flat on the bench, clamp the divider panel on top of the first panel, aligning it precisely to one side of your layout lines. Make sure the edges of both panels are flush with each other as you clamp them together. You'll only need to mark the top panel for biscuits. (See top photo, opposite page.) Remove the joiner's fence, and with the base of the joiner on the bottom panel, cut slots in the edge of the top panel by positioning the joiner to your marks. (See middle photo, opposite page.)

Without moving the setup, hold the joiner in a vertical position and cut the slots in the face of the bottom panel by aligning the base of the joiner against the edge of the top panel. Use the center mark on the base of the joiner to align the machine with your marks, as shown in the bottom left photo, opposite page.

Mark by eye. Mark for biscuit slots by dry-assembling the joint and marking across the joint line. Laying out the biscuits helps in eyeballing your marks.

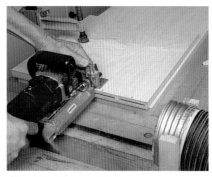

Slotting the end. Clamp the work flat and register the joiner's fence on the face of the work to make the cut. If necessary, prop up the stock so the benchtop won't interfere with the joiner's base.

Slotting the face. With the work held vertically in a vise, position the fence on the end of the work to cut the slots in the face.

Positioning the divider. Align the end of the divider to one side of your layout line, and clamp it atop and parallel with the bottom panel.

Cutting the slots. Remove or retract the fence on the joiner and register its base on the bottom panel to cut the slots in the end of the divider.

Same setup for face slots. Without altering the setup, hold the joiner vertically and register its base against the edge of the divider. Align the center mark on the joiner's base with your layout marks to cut the slots in the face.

FIG. 4 **Edge-to-Face**

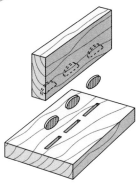

Edge-to-Face

This is a useful joint for cabinets and furniture parts, where you need to join two panels to frame pieces along the grain, such as a divider inside a case. In solid wood, the joint is plenty strong on its own without the addition of biscuits because the mating parts are both long grain. But biscuits will strengthen the joint, as well as provide an easy method for aligning the parts during assembly.

The slot-cutting technique is the same as when constructing an end-to-face joint where the panel joins in the middle of another panel, except you cut slots in the edge of one panel instead of in the end. (See opposite page.)

Good layout. On narrow work, use a small combination square on both parts to ensure your slots are precisely centered.

FIG. 5 **End-to-Edge**

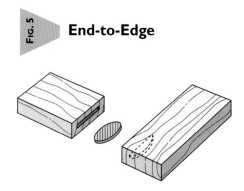

End-to-Edge

Great for cabinet frames, such as face frames or internal framework, an end-to-edge biscuit joint usually involves relatively narrow members.

Because most end-to-edge joints consist of narrow stock, it's often important to lay out the slots precisely centered on the width of the workpiece to avoid the biscuit from protruding out to one side of the joint. A good trick is to use a small combination square to locate the slot on the first piece, then use the same setting on the square to transfer the slot to the second piece, as shown in the photo, below.

Sometimes the shortest biscuit available is too long for the width of your stock. To overcome this problem

Let it stick out. On really small frames, offset the biscuit to the outside edge of the work. A centerline penciled on the biscuit helps you lay out the slots by eye.

Double Up On Biscuits

THE MAIN DRAWBACK of biscuits is their relatively short width. Although a single biscuit makes a strong joint, two or more are better. Twin biscuits located above and below each other effectively double the gluing area of any biscuit joint. A good area to use this technique is in rail joints, such as when making a table or door frame. A ³/₄-inch-thick rail can accommodate two biscuits; thicker stock will accept more biscuits. Be sure to leave sufficient material thickness on the outer cheeks of the part. I recommend a minimum thickness of ¹/₄ inch, so set the fence of the joiner to cut the first slot at that dimension or more. It's important to cut the first series of slots with the same fence setting and on the same side of your stock before adjusting the fence for the second round of slots. This ensures the joint won't bind during assembly.

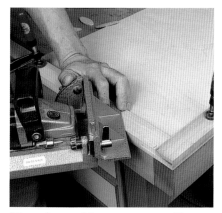

Two slots with one set-up. Clamp the two mating frame pieces to adjacent sides of a squared piece of plywood, and cut a slot in each piece by aligning the joiner to your marks.

Two are better than one. Cutting two slots for biscuits—one above the other—is an effective way to increase the gluing surface and beef up a joint.

Trim it flush. Once you've assembled the frame, trim the protruding biscuit flush using the table saw sled.

and increase the strength of the joint, you can use a large #20 biscuit in a relatively narrow frame if you allow the biscuit to extend out one side of the joint. Exposing the biscuit in this manner is a viable method for many projects, such as when building face frames for kitchen cabinets and other utilitarian casework, since the exposed biscuit is difficult to see in the finished project. Lay out the slot by dry-assembling the joint, then lay the biscuit on the stock and eyeball the slot location. (See top right photo, opposite page.)

Cutting biscuit slots in narrow stock can be awkward, and sometimes dangerous. To solve the problem, clamp a scrap piece of plywood to the bench, making sure the plywood is thinner than the frame stock and has one square corner. Clamp the frame stock to each side of the scrap at the square corner, with the end of one frame piece flush to the edge of the second piece. Now cut the slots, aligning the center mark on the joiner with the marks on your stock, as shown in the middle right photo, opposite page.

Assemble the frame, gluing the biscuits into their respective slots. Once the glue has dried, use the table saw sled to trim the protruding biscuits flush with the frame. (See bottom right photo, opposite page.)

Face-Mitered

A face-mitered biscuit joint is useful for cabinet and casework, such as making small or large boxes and bases, or for architectural trim such as mitered baseboards. Using biscuits in this type of miter joint is very effective in two ways: the biscuits register the joint, making assembly much easier, and they strengthen the inherently weak end-grain joint. The result is a corner joint with a very clean look.

Cut the miters using the table saw sled. (See middle photo, below.) Adjust the fence of your joiner to 45°, and mark the biscuit slot locations on the work. To keep the slots close to the inside, or root of the miter, use a shim if necessary under the joiner's fence to offset the slots. Plunge into the work with the piece lying flat on the bench. (See photo, below.)

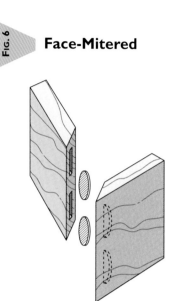

FIG. 6   **Face-Mitered**

Beveling big stuff. Large miters in case pieces are best cut on a table saw sled with the blade tilted to 45°.

Case slots. Lay out for biscuits on the inside surface of the work, then adjust the joiner's fence to 45°. A shim under the fence ensures the slots are offset towards the root of the miter for strength.

FIG. 7 **End-Mitered**

FIG. 1 **DOWEL JOINTS**

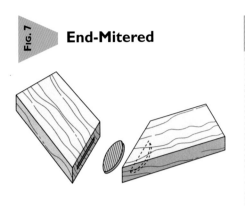

End-Mitered

This joint has many uses, typically for frame-type work such as door and case frames. Other uses include mitered edgebanding, picture frames, or architectural trim such as door casings and the like. Like the face-mitered joint, an end-mitered joint requires reinforcement to strengthen its mostly end-grain glue surfaces. Biscuits do the job with ease and efficiency.

First mark out the slots by dry-assembling the joint and striking across the center of the joint line. Then cut slots by registering the joiner's fence on the same side of all the pieces. On narrow stock, be sure to clamp the workpiece to the bench for safety.

Edge-to-Edge

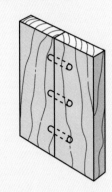

End-to-Edge

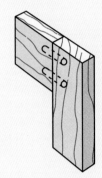

Edge-to-Face

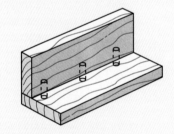

End-Mitered

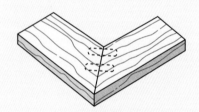

End-to-Face

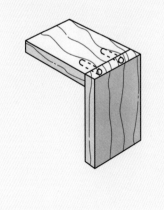

Dowel Joints

Dowel joints are one of the oldest ways of joining wood. Wooden dowels connect the parts, and they also help to line them up during assembly. Nowadays, with the increase in joinery methods, techniques, and tools, the common dowel is being replaced by more modern approaches, and therefore it isn't always the best choice for joining wood. It is still a standard joint for mass-produced furniture in factories equipped with industrial doweling machines. However, because a dowel joint is relatively simple and easy to accomplish, it's still a good choice in small shops for many situations, especially for the beginner and for those of us with limited power tools.

Dowels can be made in a range of diameters from a variety of materials, including commercial dowels, hardwood rods, or even bamboo sticks or pins. Interestingly, Chinese craftsmen have been using bamboo pins in woodworking joints for many centuries. Be sure to select your dowel stock before cutting the joints. (See Choosing Dowels, next page.)

Accurate drilling is the key to making accurate dowel joints, and you have two options for most joints. You can use the drill press, or you can use a hand drill with the aid of doweling jigs. Regardless of the approach you take, be sure to use brad-point bits when drilling the dowel holes for clean, accurate holes. (For more on brad-point bits, see Hand Drills and the Drill Press, page 14.)

Edge-to-Edge

This joint is typically used when making larger panels from smaller pieces. In this particular case, the dowels themselves will strengthen the joint, but are primarily used for alignment purposes. That's because the long-grain to long-grain gluing area of the joint is sufficiently strong by itself. Nevertheless, it makes sense to add dowels for easing the glue-up process by helping to keep the boards level with each other. Preparing the joint is very much the same as creating an edge-to-edge butt joint (see Butt Joints, page 43), where smooth, straight edges are essential.

The first step to making an edge-to-edge dowel joint is to use the jointer or the table saw to machine the edges of your stock dead straight. Once the boards fit tightly together, you can use a hand drill or the drill press to drill the holes for the dowels.

With a hand drill. Drilling by hand is probably the most effective method for making an edge-to-edge joint, especially for really wide stock. Mark the boards for the dowels, spacing the dowels every 6 inches or so. Then use a doweling jig clamped to the work to drill the holes. (See Doweling Jigs, page 33.)

On the drill press. The challenge when using the drill press for drilling dowel holes in the edge of work is when you're faced with relatively wide stock. Keeping the stock at 90° to the bit can be a chore. Use a tall fence to register the work (see Bandsaw/Drill Press Fence, page 35). Clamp the fence to the drill press table such that bit is aligned with the center of the stock. Then mark your centers for the dowel holes, set the depth stop on the press,

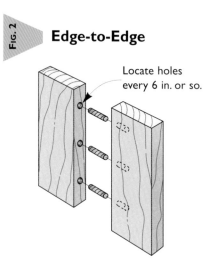

Fig. 2 ▶ Edge-to-Edge

Locate holes every 6 in. or so.

and drill all your holes in one board. For the mating piece, be sure to register the same face against the fence so any slight discrepancies won't affect the alignment of the boards.

Choosing Dowels

THERE ARE SEVERAL choices when it comes to choosing dowels for dowel joints. Commercially made dowels are available in a wide range of diameters, typically $1/4$, $5/16$, $3/8$, and $1/2$ inch, or even larger. Commercial dowels are grooved in either a spiral or fluted pattern. The grooves allow trapped air to escape when the dowel is inserted in the hole, making assembly easier.

A less-expensive alternative is to make your own dowels from hardwood dowel rods. Be sure to check the rod's actual size, since a dowel rod is sometimes slightly under or over the nominal diameter. After cutting the dowels to the correct length, I like to compress them between two boards placed in a bench vise. This makes the dowels fit easily into their respective holes, and allows them to swell when the glue is applied, making a strong joint.

Another convenient material for dowel stock is $1/8$-inch bamboo skewer. You can pick them up in packs at the supermarket. Bamboo has a very strong fiber structure that makes it ideal for small dowels.

It's important to choose the correct length of dowel for the joint you're making. Generally, longer is better. For example, I use a 2-inch dowel for a typical edge-to-face joint in $3/4$-inch material, where about $1/2$ inch of the dowel goes into the face-grain piece, and the remaining $1 1/4$ inch goes into the edge-grain member.

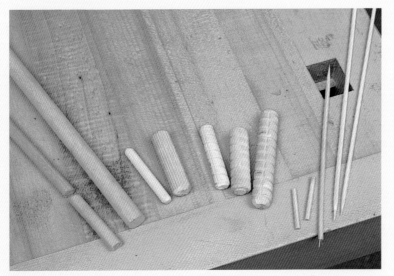

Dowel types. From left to right: hardwood dowel rods; fluted dowels; spiral-grooved dowels; and bamboo skewers.

FIG. 3

Edge-to-Face

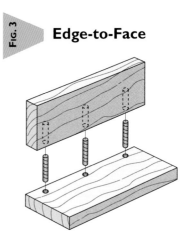

Edge-to-Face

An edge-to-face dowel joint is typically used in cabinet construction and casework, where a panel or frame piece joins another at right angles. Adding dowels to the joint is great for registering the parts, although the joint is strong enough without the dowels since the glued surfaces are both long grain. The process uses a hand drill or can be done on the drill press.

With a hand drill. You'll need a doweling jig for accurate drilling of the dowel holes. (See Doweling Jigs, page 33.) Prepare the stock with flat and straight surfaces, then align the parts and mark them for the dowel holes. Dowels should be spaced every 6 inches or so. Clamp the doweling jig to the work and drill the holes, referencing the jig on each outside face of the mating boards.

On the drill press. A drill press and fence will make short work of drilling the holes for this joint, as long as the workpiece is relatively narrow. (For wide work, you'll need to support the stock on edge with the bandsaw/drill press fence shown on page 25). The operation for drilling the face board

Drill fence and stop. Equipping your drill press with a fence and a depth stop makes drilling accurate dowel holes easy, especially in multiple workpieces.

and the edge board are identical. Mark the locations of the dowel holes on your stock, then clamp a fence to the drill press table to register the work to the bit. Set the depth stop on the press to the desired depth of the holes, then use steady feed pressure as you drill. (See photo, above.)

FIG. 4

End-to-Face

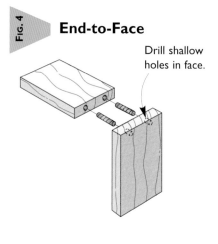

Drill shallow holes in face.

End-to-Face

This joint relies on dowels for strength as well as alignment. Typical applications are for furniture and cabinetwork, where corners come together. Either a hand drill or the drill press can be used to construct this joint.

With a hand drill. Use a doweling jig (see page 33). Bore slightly deeper holes in the end-grain piece for added strength, but be sure to bore shallower holes in the face piece so they don't blow through the back side. A piece of tape wrapped around the drill bit will act as a depth guide. (See top photo, right.)

On the drill press. You have two options for drilling the end-grain member. If your drill press table tilts, adjust it vertically and clamp the workpiece to the table. (See photo, right.) If your table can't pivot, you can clamp the bandsaw/drill press fence (see page 25) vertically to the drill table, then clamp the workpiece to the fence. (See top photo, next page.)

Drilling the holes in the face piece is easy, even if the workpiece is particularly wide. Simply mark for the holes, set the depth stop on your drill press, and drill. If the drill press column

Drill guide and tape. Clamp the doweling jig securely to the stock and use a piece of tape wrapped around the bit to flag the hole depth.

Tilt the table. Holes in long stock are best drilled with the table positioned parallel with the bit. Clamp the workpiece in place, then adjust the table by aligning the bit with the edge of the work.

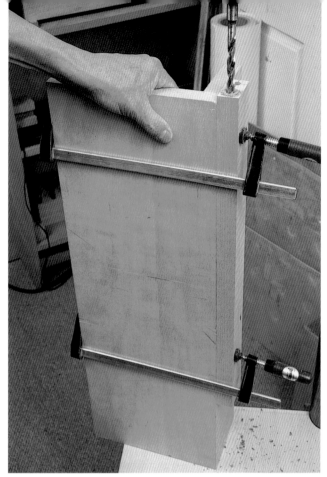

Tall fence for support. If your drill press table doesn't pivot, an alternative is to clamp a long fence to the table for supporting stock when drilling into end grain.

First one side, then the other. On wide work, drill from both sides so the stock clears the drill press post.

limits the cut, drill all the holes on one half of the panel, then reorient the stock 180° on the table and drill the remaining holes, as shown in the photo, above.

FIG. 5

End-to-Edge

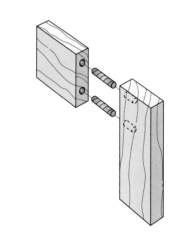

End-to-Edge

Probably the most common dowel joint used in woodworking, an end-to-edge joint is useful in furniture and cabinet work where you need to make frames, from flat face and door frames to three-dimensional frames, such as the framework for a chair where two seat rails meet a leg. Both the drill press and a hand drill can be used for making this joint.

With a hand drill. Use a doweling jig (see page 33) with your drill and bit to drill the dowel holes. Mark the stock for dowels by positioning the parts as they will meet in the finished joint, then drill the holes in the individual members. Drill the end-grain holes with the doweling jig clamped to the end of the piece, then use the same jig clamped to the long-grain member to drill the opposing holes, aligning the jig with your marks as shown in the photos on the opposite page.

On the drill press. Boring the dowel holes on the drill press for an end-to-edge joint is the same technique you use when constructing an end-to-face joint. (See End-to-Face, previous page.) Mark your dowel hole locations, then drill the end-grain holes with the stock clamped vertically to the drill press table, or use the bandsaw/drill press fence (see page 25) to register the stock at right angles to the bit. Drill the holes on the edge of the mating member by standing the stock on edge and registering it against a fence clamped to the drill press table.

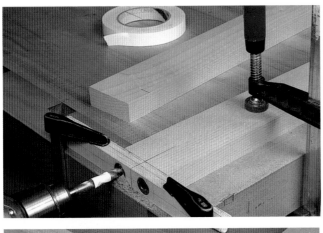

End and side grain. Use the same doweling jig to drill for dowel holes in both parts, clamping the jig against the end grain and to your layout mark on the first piece (top), then repositioning the same jig on the side of the second piece (above).

FIG. 6 **End-Mitered**

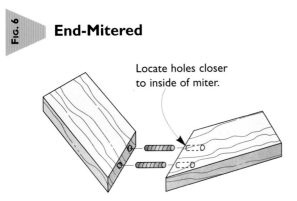

Locate holes closer to inside of miter.

Staggering Dowels

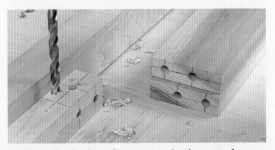

WHEN YOU'RE faced with dowel joints in three planes, such as where two rails or two panels join to a post, you'll need to find a way to avoid having the dowels intersect and hit each other inside the post. The trick is to stagger your dowel holes, which makes glue-up easier and keeps the post strong because all the holes aren't drilled at the same spot.

Offset the holes. Staggering the layout of your dowels holes lets you maximize the amount of dowels you can use without causing interference.

End-Mitered

Like the end-to-edge joint dowel joint, a 45° face miter is useful for framework and other areas where two miters meet. This joint is mostly end grain, so it pays to add dowels to strengthen the connection. While you can drill for dowels using the drill press, the process is complicated. You're better off using a hand drill and a doweling jig.

With a hand drill. Use a doweling jig (see page 33) to help with boring accurate holes in both miters. First hold the joint together and mark for the dowel holes, making sure to keep the holes as close to the root of the miter as possible for strength. Then clamp the drilling jig to the face of each miter, and drill straight into the stock. This way, the dowel holes will be in line with each other when you assemble the parts.

FIG. I

RABBET JOINTS

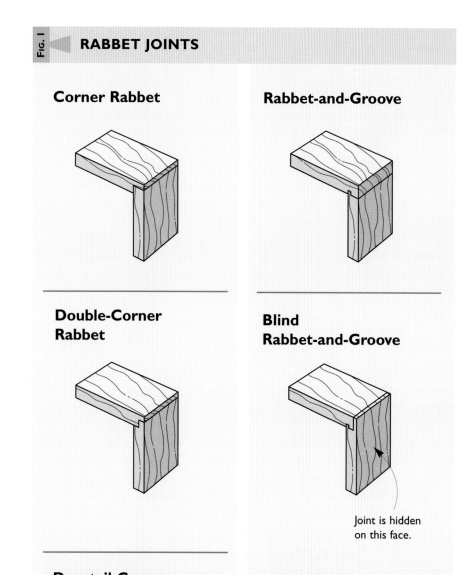

Corner Rabbet

Rabbet-and-Groove

Double-Corner Rabbet

Blind Rabbet-and-Groove

Joint is hidden on this face.

Dovetail-Corner Rabbet

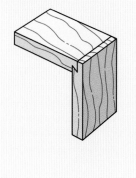

Rabbet Joints

In joining a board on edges or ends, one method is to use rabbet joints. A standard rabbet is a step cut into the edge or end of a workpiece, usually half the thickness of the stock. The adjoining member is then fit into the rabbet. This joint is used in building cabinets, boxes, and drawers. Though it is not as visually appealing as a dovetail joint, a rabbet joint is very practical and simple and can be made without special tools or jigs. The rabbet itself offers positive alignment and simplifies glue-up and assembly. Plus, joints are reinforced because the shoulder resists racking.

Most rabbet joints can be cut on the table saw with a standard blade or a dado cutter, on the router table, or with a hand-held router equipped with an edge guide. Another option is to use bearing-guided rabbetting bits in the router. (See Bearings Determine the Cut, page 78.)

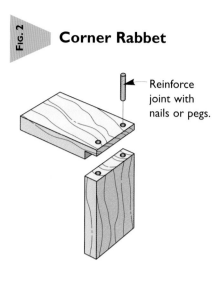

Fig. 2

Corner Rabbet

Reinforce joint with nails or pegs.

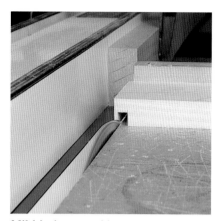

Nibble it away. Use a single saw blade and a table saw sled to cut a rabbet, making repeated passes to remove the waste. A block clamped to the fence determines the rabbet's length.

Stand it up. After cutting the first cheek with the miter gauge, rip the second cheek to complete the rabbet by clamping the stock to the tenoning jig.

Corner Rabbet

The most basic of all rabbet joints, a corner rabbet is a standard joint for corners on casework and other box-type construction, including drawers. Since the joint doesn't lock mechanically, it's best to reinforce the parts with dowel pins or nails. You can make the joint on the table saw, router table, or with a hand-held router.

On the table saw. The table saw is very efficient for cutting rabbet joints. A standard single blade will do a respectable job of cutting this joint, but you'll have to make repeated passes. There are two approaches. The first involves laying the stock flat on the single-runner table saw sled (see page 20). Set the blade height to the desired depth of the rabbet (taking into account the base of the sled) and clamp a stop block to the rip fence, forward of the blade. With the work on the sled and one end against the stop, set the rip fence to the finished length of the rabbet. Make repeated passes over the saw blade until the work contacts the stop. (See top middle photo, above.)

The second method using a standard blade is to incorporate the tenoning jig (see page 23) into the cutting action. First, set the blade height just shy of the finished depth of the rabbet, and adjust the rip fence so the blade cuts to the exact rabbet length. Use the miter gauge to push the stock over the blade. Then clamp the workpiece to the tenoning jig and adjust the rip fence until the blade is aligned with the finished depth of the rabbet. The height of the blade should equal the finished rabbet length. Now push the work over the blade, removing a strip of waste to create the rabbet. (See top right photo, above.)

A dado blade is more effective for removing the waste when cutting a rabbet, allowing you to form a rabbet in one pass. On narrow stock, use the double-runner sled (see page 21) and a stop block clamped to the sled's fence to make the cut. Make sure to account for the thickness of the sled's base when setting the height of the blade. Use the same procedure for rabbetting wide stock, as shown in the photos, right.

Wide or narrow. A dado blade makes quick work of milling rabbets. Use a stop block to register the work (top). Even big panels can be rabbetted using the same setup (above).

On the router table. Install a rabbeting bit (see Bearings Determine the Cut below, right) in the router table, and set the fence to the desired rabbet length, or flush with the bit's bearing. Set the bit height equal to the finished rabbet depth, and run the work past the bit. (See photo, below.) If the workpiece is relatively narrow (less than 6 inches or so), be sure to use a suitable push block behind the work to guide it and help keep it from tipping into the bit.

Another option is to use a regular straight bit for cutting the rabbet. Use the same setup as the rabbetting bit, setting the fence for the length of the rabbet. Select your biggest diameter bit for the cleanest cut.

With a hand-held router. Install a bearing-guided rabbet bit (see Bearings Determine the Cut, below) in your router, making sure the bearing is the correct diameter for the desired length of the rabbet. Set the depth of cut (it's best to make a test cut on some scrap), then rout the rabbet with the workpiece firmly clamped. To avoid blowout, clamp a scrap piece at the back of the workpiece. (See bottom left photo, below.)

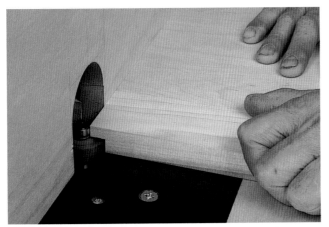

Rabbet on a bearing. A piloted rabbeting bit makes cutting a rabbet on the router table simple by letting the workpiece ride the bearing. Use a piece of wide scrap to guide narrow work.

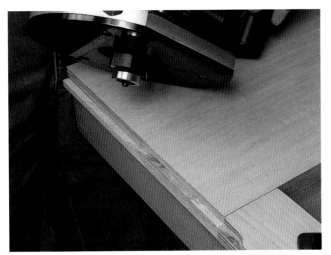

Rabbet by hand. Use a bearing-guided bit in a hand-held router for quick and accurate rabbets. Scrap clamped at the end of the cut prevents tearout on the workpiece.

Bearings Determine the Cut

SEVERAL router bit manufacturers offer a rabbeting set, which comes with a standard rabbetting bit and a host of replaceable bearings. The bearings come in a variety of diameters. You pick the right size of bearing for the rabbet you need to cut and secure it to the bit. By guiding the work against the bearing, either with a hand-held router or on the router table, you can rout the precise length of rabbet you need without worrying about fence adjustments.

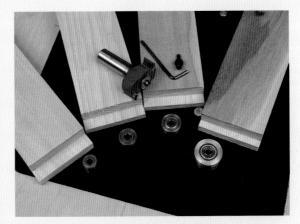

Small bearing equals longer rabbet. By varying the diameter of your bearings you can tailor the desired length of the rabbet.

Double-Corner Rabbet

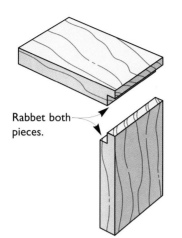

Rabbet both pieces.

Dovetail-Corner Rabbet

Half tail

Double-Corner Rabbet

This is a very similar joint to the basic corner rabbet, except both pieces are rabbetted. The result is a joint with more strength because of the increased gluing surface. Like the single corner rabbet, the joint is great for casework and other box-type construction. Again, it's best to add dowel pins or nails after gluing the joint for reinforcement. You can make the joint on the table saw, router table, or with a hand-held router.

On the table saw. See corner rabbet (see page 77) for the cutting procedure. The only difference here is that you need to rabbet both parts. It's best to cut the rabbet on one part first, then cut the second rabbet to fit the first.

On the router table. Use the same procedure for routing this joint as you did for the corner rabbet (See page 77). Make sure to rabbet both parts, cutting the rabbet in one part and then cutting the second rabbet to fit the first.

With a hand-held router. Again, use the same technique for routing the corner rabbet (see page 77). Rout the rabbet in one part, then rout the second rabbet to fit the first.

Dovetail-Corner Rabbet

A dovetailed corner rabbet adds an interesting twist to an otherwise common joint, in that the rabbetted ledge of one part and the tongue of the adjoining member come together at a slope, or dovetail angle. The effect is to create a mechanical link, since the sloping connections prevent the joint from coming apart in one direction. It is still best to reinforce this joint with dowels or pins, especially on wide stock. But the dovetailed joint has more strength than a standard corner rabbet. While it's possible to cut this joint on the table saw by tilting the saw blade, the best method is to use a dovetail bit on the router table.

On the router table. Chuck a dovetail bit in the router, and install a zero-clearance fence. (See page 29.) Set the bit height equal to the thickness of the blind member (the part that will overlap the adjoining member), and adjust the fence until the bit cuts a full slope on the workpiece. Make a test cut to ensure your setup is correct. Rout the first piece with the stock held vertically, using a back-up board to guide the cut and to prevent blowout. (See top left photo, next page.)

Vertical cut. Use a dovetail bit in the router table to cut one half of the joint. A wide block steadies the work and prevents tearout at the back of the cut.

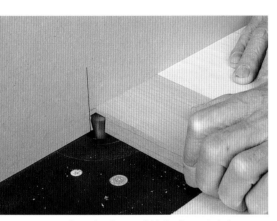

Lay it down. With the work lying flat and without altering the bit height, use the same dovetail bit to rout the opposite half of the joint. Another back-up block guides the work and prevents blowout.

Using the same bit, rout the second piece with the stock flat on the table. Don't alter the bit height. Adjust the fence until the top, or widest part of the bit, equals the thickness of the first piece. Again, use a back-up block to guide the work—particularly if it's relatively narrow—and to prevent tearing or blowing out the back of the joint. (See photo, above.)

Rabbet-and-Groove

For maximum strength, a rabbet-and-groove joint adds a tongue formed by the rabbet that locks into a groove in the adjoining member. This joint can be glued without reinforcing fasteners. Accurately fitting the tongue to the groove is the key to a good joint. All three machines—the table saw, the router table, or a hand-held router—work fine for cutting this joint. One note: For maximum strength, make the groove (and its corresponding tongue) as deep as it is wide.

On the table saw. Whenever possible, cut the groove first so you can fit the tongue to it. Set the blade height to the depth of the groove, and use the miter gauge or a table saw sled to push the stock over the blade. (When using a sled, be sure to account for the thickness of its base when setting the blade height.) The work should ride against the rip fence such that one side of the groove falls on the joint line.

Form the tongue as you would an ordinary corner rabbet (see page 77), by either running the work horizontally

FIG. 5

Rabbet-and-Groove

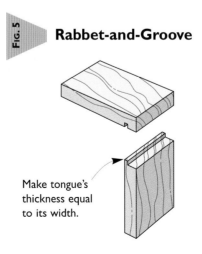

Make tongue's thickness equal to its width.

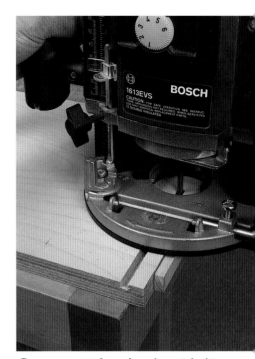

Groove near the edge. A straight bit and an edge guide secured to the router lets you cut an accurate groove.

on the single-runner sled or by clamping the stock vertically in the tenoning jig. One pass with a standard blade should do the job if your tongue is ⅛ inch thick.

On the router table. Install a straight bit in the router, and adjust the height to the desired groove depth. Lay the workpiece flat on the table and use a back-up block to guide the work past the bit. Cut the rabbet to fit the groove by following the same procedure for cutting a corner rabbet (see page 77).

With a hand-held router. Cut the groove by installing a straight bit in the router, then guiding the cut with an edge guide. (See photo, above)

Cut the rabbet and its tongue to fit the groove with a rabbetting bit, using the same technique for the basic corner rabbet (see page 77).

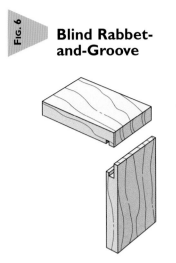

FIG. 6

Blind Rabbet-and-Groove

Blind Rabbet-and-Groove

For maximum strength and good looks, a blind rabbet-and-groove is a good choice. When the joint is assembled, the show side of the joint (usually the face of a case piece or the front of a drawer) is hidden. Like the standard rabbet-and-groove, the success of this joint hinges on a tongue that fits the groove precisely. You can use the table saw or the router table to construct this joint.

On the table saw. Start by plowing a notch in the end of the show piece. Use a standard saw blade or a dado blade, and clamp the work vertically against the tenoning jig (see page 23). You can make the cut in one pass with a dado blade; a single blade will require that you reset the rip fence and make multiple passes. Set the blade height equal to the thickness of the adjoining piece, and center the notch on the stock. (See photo, below.)

Next, shorten one of the tongues by laying the stock flat on the saw table and pushing it past the blade with the miter gauge. Clamp or screw a scrap fence to your miter gauge to guide the workpiece, and clamp a stop block to the fence to register the work, as shown in the photo, right. Remember to mill the tongue's length equal to its thickness.

Use the milled tongue to lay out the location of the groove. (See bottom right photo, below.) Then cut the groove in the adjoining member as you would when making a standard rabbet-

and-groove (see opposite page), using the miter gauge or a table saw sled.

On the router table. Chuck a straight bit in the router, and set the bit height equal to the thickness of the non-show piece. Adjust the fence so the bit is centered on the thickness of the show piece, then rout a notch in the end of the piece by standing the stock upright

Trim one tongue. Shorten the inside tongue using the miter gauge fitted with a long fence. A stop block registers the end of the stock.

Notch it first. Plow a wide, centered notch in the end with a dado blade by clamping the work vertically against the tenoning jig.

Mark for the groove. Use the milled tongue to lay out the groove location, making a tick mark with the point of a knife.

Tall routing. Rout the notch in one pass using a straight bit in the router table. Use a tall fence, and steady the work with a featherboard and a wide push block.

and guiding it with a push block. (See photo, above.) Cut the tongue to finished length by repositioning the fence and laying the stock flat on the table. (You may need to lower the bit height, depending on the stock you're working with.) Push the stock over the bit, using a back-up block if the stock is narrow, as shown in the photo, below.

Finish the joint by routing the groove in the adjoining member, using the same technique for routing a standard rabbet-and-groove.

Rout the tongue. With the same bit, trim the tongue to length by registering the work against the fence. Use a wide push block for safety.

FIG. I

DADO JOINTS

Through Dado

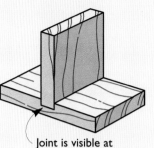

Joint is visible at front and back.

Dado-and-Rabbet

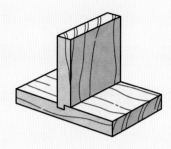

Stopped Dado

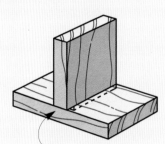

Joint is hidden at front.

Dado-and-Tongue

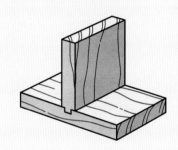

Blind Dado

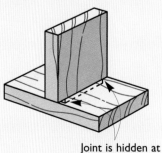

Joint is hidden at front and back.

Dado Joints

A dado joint strengthens parts, and also helps to align them during assembly. You'll find this joint in cabinet construction, typically where shelves join sides, such as in bookcase construction. In a dado joint, a groove is cut across the workpiece, and the mating workpiece is then fit to the groove. There are different ways to make the end of the adjoining piece fit the groove, from rabbetted, tongued, or stopped dadoes.

Most dado joints can be cut quite easily on a table saw, or with a handheld router accompanied by a dado jig (see page 26). While it's possible to cut the joint on the router table, you're better off using a hand-held router for mid-size and big workpieces (which account for most dado joints) because it's much easier and more accurate to move the router instead of moving the work.

Through Dado

The through-dado joint is the most common and utilitarian of all dado joints. You'll find this joint on many cabinets, typically when joining a top, bottom, or shelf to the sides of a case. The joint can be cut on the table saw or with a hand-held router.

On the table saw. Mark the dado locations on the edge of your stock, then set up a dado blade equal to the width of your desired dado. Use paper shims if necessary to adjust the width so the dado cut fits the mating piece precisely. With the double-runner sled (see page 21) on your saw table, adjust the height of the blade to equal the finished depth of the dado. Place the stock against the sled's fence, line up your layout marks with the blade, and push the stock and sled over the blade to make the cut. (See bottom left photo, below.)

With a hand-held router. Use the dado jig (see page 26) and a straight bit in your router to make the cut. Set the

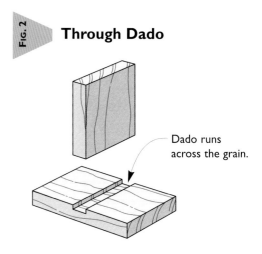

Fig. 2 **Through Dado**

Dado runs across the grain.

depth of cut directly from the base plate of your router. The jig simplifies layout: Just mark one side of the dado location on the stock, then clamp the jig to your mark. It's a good idea to use a square to check that the jig is square to the work. When you're satisfied with the setup, guide the router on the right side of the jig and push it away from you to rout the dado, as shown in the photo, below.

Table saw dadoes. Line up the edge of the dado blade with your layout marks, and plow the dado in one pass using a table saw sled.

Jig makes it straight. Use a straight bit and the dado jig clamped to the work to rout a dado. For really deep dadoes, make successive cuts until you reach the full depth.

Determining Dado Depth

DADOES SHOULDN'T BE too deep, or they can weaken the joint area. While a deeper cut can increase the gluing area of the joint, a dado's main purpose is to accurately locate the adjoining workpiece. Generally, dadoes that are 1/8 to 3/16 inch deep in solid wood are sufficient for strength. A little deeper dado—about 1/4 inch—is best for plywood or MDF. Another benefit of keeping your dadoes relatively shallow is that you'll end up with thicker stock underneath the dado itself. This lets you use fasteners, such as nails or screws, more securely since the fasteners will hold better in thicker stock.

FIG. 3   Determining Dado Depth

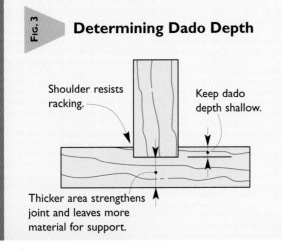

Shoulder resists racking.

Keep dado depth shallow.

Thicker area strengthens joint and leaves more material for support.

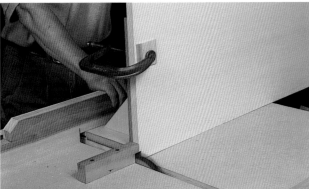

Safe notches. A table saw sled and a tall fence makes cutting a notch with a dado blade easier on your nerves. Screw or clamp a tall fence to the sled, and use a stop block screwed to the sled to register the work.

Stopped Dado

Like the through dado, the stopped-dado joint is useful in cabinet construction. A stopped dado results in a joint that's invisible from the front, a handy feature if you need to conceal the joinery in a piece. You can use a table saw to cut this joint, but it's easiest to make the stopped cut with a hand-held plunge router.

On the table saw. Cut the dado in the workpiece using the same technique as when cutting a through dado (see previous page), but stop the cut about 1/4 to 1/2 inch from the edge of the work. You can make this stopped cut by clamping a stop block on the table of your saw. Finish the stopped dado by squaring up the curve at the end of the cut with a sharp chisel.

To cut the notch in the adjoining piece, use the double-runner sled (see page 21) with the bandsaw/drill press fence (see page 25) attached to the base of the sled. Screw a stop block to the sled's base, then clamp the workpiece on edge against the fence and cut the notch by running the assembly over the blade. (See photo, below.)

With a hand-held router. The dado half of this joint is easily cut with a hand-held plunge router and a straight bit utilizing the dado jig (see page 26). To cut the notch in the adjoining workpiece, see the table saw technique above. Set the depth of cut for the desired dado, measuring directly from the router's baseplate. Mark one side of the dado location on the stock, then clamp the jig to your mark. You can rout the stopped dado freehand by stopping at a mark on the workpiece. For more accuracy, it's best to clamp a stop block to the jig itself. Position the block so the router's baseplate contacts the stop at the correct location on the work, then plunge the bit into the work, guiding the router against the jig. The setup is similar to routing a blind dado, as shown in the bottom photo, opposite page.

FIG. 4   Stopped Dado

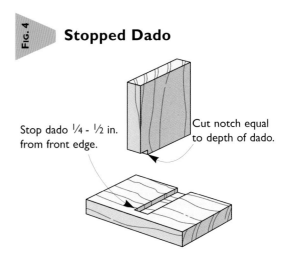

Stop dado 1/4 - 1/2 in. from front edge.

Cut notch equal to depth of dado.

Routing Angled Dadoes

YOU CAN MAKE all sorts of angled dadoes—through and stopped—using an angled dado jig (see page 26) and a straight bit in your router. Once you've made the jig, find the desired angle of your dadoes and adjust the jig to that angle. Mark one side of each dado location on the stock, and set the router bit to cut the desired depth, measuring from the router's baseplate. Clamp the jig securely to the mark, and simply push the router away from you and along the right side of the jig.

Easy angles. The angled dado jig simplifies cutting angled dadoes, whether through or stopped. Use a straight bit and clamp the jig so its working edge is at the required distance from your layout marks.

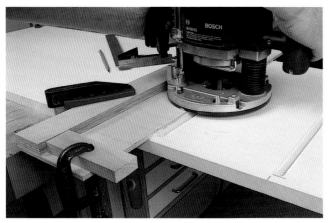

Stopping the cut. Clamp stop blocks at the ends of the dado jig to limit the router's travel when routing a stopped dado.

Blind Dado

Similar to a stopped dado is the blind-dado joint. The difference is that a blind dado is stopped on both sides of the work, so you won't see the dado itself on either side when the joint is assembled. This is a handy joint when a clean look is desired, such as when joining shelves to case sides or doing other high-end cabinet construction. A hand-held router accompanied by the dado jig (see page 26) is the best approach to cutting this joint.

With a hand-held router. Use a similar technique as when routing a stopped dado, except you must stop the cut at both ends, and you need to cut a shoulder on all four sides of the adjoining member.

Rout the dado first, using a plunge router equipped with a straight bit and guided by the dado jig. Use a stop block clamped at each end of the jig to stop the cut. Plunge the bit into the work, stopping when the router's baseplate contacts the stops on the jig, as shown in the bottom left photo, below.

You can cut the shoulders in the adjoining stock in a variety of ways. It helps if you think of the process as cutting away the shoulders to form a stub tenon or tongue. You can use the table saw and a table saw sled to cut the shoulders as you would when cutting an edge-to-edge tongue-and-groove joint (see page 47). Or, chuck a rabbetting bit in your router and rout a rabbet on all four edges to form the tongue. (See Rabbet Joints, page 76.) Make sure the tongue fits securely in the dado and that the shoulders make full contact with the face of the adjoining piece.

FIG. 5

Blind Dado

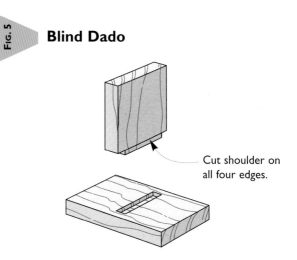

Cut shoulder on all four edges.

FIG. 6

Dado-and-Rabbet

FIG. 7

Dado-and-Tongue

FIG. I

FINGER JOINTS

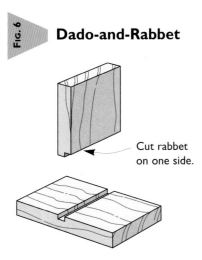

Cut rabbet on one side.

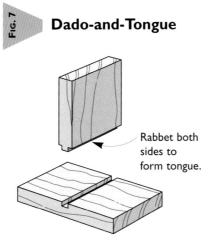

Rabbet both sides to form tongue.

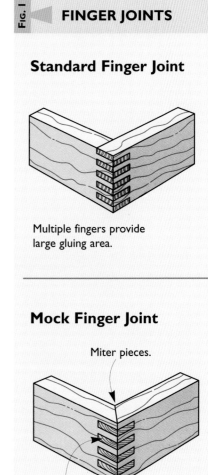

Standard Finger Joint

Multiple fingers provide large gluing area.

Mock Finger Joint

Miter pieces.

Mock finger

Dado-and-Rabbet

This joint is easy to make, and can be used for the same applications as when using a through dado, such as when joining case parts. The difference here is that the extra shoulder provides a little more glue surface and helps to prevent the joint from racking. You can make this joint on the table saw, or with a hand-held router and the dado jig (see page 26).

On the table saw. Cut the dado first using the same technique as for milling a through dado (see page 83), using a dado blade with the stock flat on the double-runner sled (see page 21). Next, mill the rabbet on the adjoining member, positioning the stock flat on the sled and adjusting the height of the dado blade so the tongue fits the dado securely. A stop block screwed to the sled limits the cut for the correct length of the rabbet.

With a hand-held router. Use the dado jig to rout the dado in the first piece, using the same method as when routing a through dado (see page 83). Then rabbet the second piece using a rabbetting bit equipped with a ball bearing. (See Rabbet Joints, page 76.)

Dado-and-Tongue

This joint is very similar to a dado-and-rabbet, except you form shoulders on both sides of the work. The extra shoulder will help hide glue lines, and is handy when you need a very clean-looking joint. Both the table saw and a hand-held router can be used to make this joint.

On the table saw. Mill the dado as you would an ordinary through dado (see page 83). Use the double-runner sled (see page 21) and the desired width of dado blade in the saw. Then cut the shoulders on the adjoining piece by positioning the stock flat on the sled, using a stop block screwed to the sled to limit the cut to the correct rabbet length. Be sure to mill both sides of the stock to form the tongue.

With a hand-held router. Use the dado jig (see page 26) to rout the dado, using the same method as when routing a through dado (see page 83). Then rabbet both sides of the adjoining piece using a rabbetting bit equipped with a ball bearing. (See Rabbet Joints, page 76.)

Finger Joints

Finger joints are most commonly associated with drawers, where they make a strong connection at the four corners of the box and are attractive as well. But larger boxes, such as pedestals and cabinets, can benefit from this joint, too. The multiple, interlocking fingers allow for a large total gluing area, making this joint very strong. One variation, the mock-finger joint, is actually a miter joint fitted with wooden pins. The advantage of this joint over the standard finger joint is that you can choose any variety of wood for the pins as a decorative feature.

Finger joints can be made on the table saw using the miter gauge and a special jig. (See fig. 3, Finger Joint Jig.) The same jig lets you cut the joint very accurately using the router table and the sliding fence jig (see page 29).

FIG. 2

Standard Finger Joint

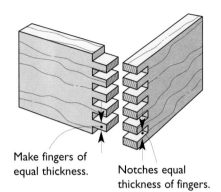

Make fingers of equal thickness.

Notches equal thickness of fingers.

Standard Finger Joint

This joint is used to construct boxes, often in cabinets, but more typically for drawers. The finger joint is easy to make, and it has good visual appeal, similar to a through-dovetail joint (see page 140). You'll need a special jig for making this joint, as shown in figure 3. You can use the jig on the table saw or on the router table.

One tip: Be sure to lay out the spacing of the fingers and notches on your stock so you end up with full-size fingers or notches on both edges of the work, by either ripping the stock to the correct width or by adjusting the width of the fingers themselves. Usually, it's best to lay out an odd number of fingers so you'll get matching cuts at each edge.

On the table saw. Install a dado blade on the saw, equal in width to the desired fingers. Position the double-runner sled (see page 21) on the saw table, then adjust the height of the blade to the length of the fingers, taking into account the sled's base. Now clamp the finger-joint jig to the sled's fence. Make a test cut in scrap to align the locating stick at the correct distance from the blade. Cut a full notch

First cut. Use the finger joint jig clamped to the table saw sled to mill finger joints. Make the first cut by positioning the work against the edge of the stick.

FIG. 3

Finger Joint Jig

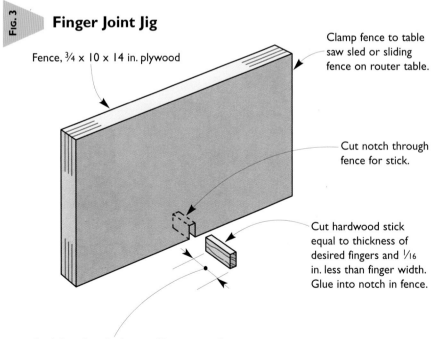

Fence, ¾ x 10 x 14 in. plywood

Clamp fence to table saw sled or sliding fence on router table.

Cut notch through fence for stick.

Cut hardwood stick equal to thickness of desired fingers and ¹⁄₁₆ in. less than finger width. Glue into notch in fence.

Stick length = thickness of fence + stock

Notches on a stick. Cut the remaining notches by placing the previous notch over the stick.

Open notch. Mill the fingers in the mating board by starting with a notch cut on the edge of the board.

in the first workpiece by aligning the workpiece upright against the fence and the edge of the stick. (See bottom photo, previous page.) Continue cutting the remaining notches in the first board by inserting the previously cut notch over the stick, as shown in the photo, left.

Cut the notches in the adjoining board to correspond to the fingers in the first board. Start by cutting an open notch on one edge of the stock. To do this, hold the board one notch width away from the stick, or flush with one side of the blade. (See middle left photo, below.) Then cut the remaining notches using the same technique as before, registering the previously-cut notch over the stick.

On the router table. To rout a finger joint, you use the same technique for cutting the notches as on the table saw, as described above. On the router table, install the sliding fence (see page 29), then clamp the finger-joint jig to the fence. As before, cut all the notches in the first workpiece, starting with a full notch, then registering the previous notch on the jig's stick to rout successive notches. (See bottom left photo, below.) Then rout all the notches in the mating piece with the same setup, aligning the first notch flush with the side of the blade.

Routing fingers. Use the finger joint jig clamped to the sliding fence for routing finger joints. The stick registers the work for evenly-spaced fingers.

FIG. 4

Mock Finger Joint

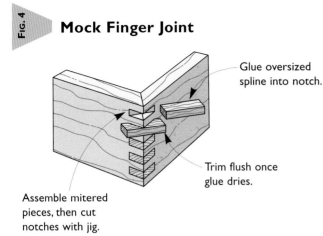

Glue oversized spline into notch.

Trim flush once glue dries.

Assemble mitered pieces, then cut notches with jig.

height to this second line, as shown in the photo, below.

Holding one corner of the work in the cradle jig, push the work over the spinning bit to cut the notches. Layout lines on the jig itself establish the correct notch spacing. (See bottom photo, below.)

Mock-Finger Joint

As its name indicates, the mock finger joint is not a true finger joint, but technically a face-mitered spine joint with "fingers" or splines for reinforcement. The fun part of this joint is that you can make the splines from different varieties and colors of wood as an accent, making any project more appealing and interesting.

The first step in constructing this joint is to miter and assemble the parts as you would for a face-mitered spline joint, without cutting the slots for splines (see page 59). Once you've cut the miters, glue and clamp the boards together. You can construct the joint on the table saw or the router table, using the cradle jig (see page 30). After installing the splines, use the bandsaw to trim the excess as close as possible to the sides of the workpiece. Then flush them up with a plane, working from the corners inward to avoid breaking the delicate end-grain fibers.

On the table saw. Follow the same procedure used for making the joint on the router table (see below), securing the work in the cradle jig. The only differences here are that you use a dado blade to cut the notches, and you use the rip fence to guide the cradle jig, moving the fence for each cut to register the correct notch spacing.

On the router table. Install a straight bit in the router, and position the cradle jig on the table. For the best-looking joint, make the fingers equal in length to the thickness of the work. Do this by marking a square line across the edge of the work from an inside corner, then drawing a 45° line across the miter joint from your mark with a combination square. Set the bit

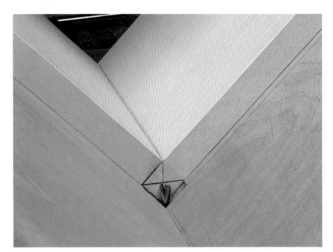

Set the bit height. To make the fingers equal to the thickness of the work, line up the bit to a 45° line drawn across the miter joint.

Cradle your work. Line up the edge of the workpiece with lines penciled on the jig to rout equally spaced notches.

FIG. 1 ◄ **LAP JOINTS**

Shiplap

Corner Lap

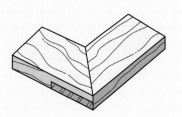

Half-Blind Lap

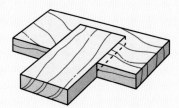

Half-Lap

Boards are
equal thickness.

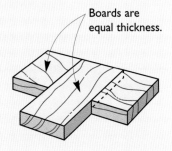

Mitered-Corner Lap

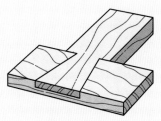

Dovetail Lap

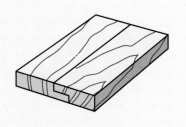

Full Lap

Thinner board;
usually by half.

Angled Lap

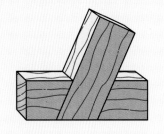

Keyed-Dovetail Lap

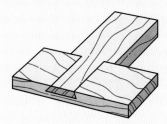

Bridle Joint

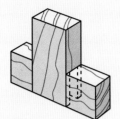

VARIATION

Long and Deep Lap

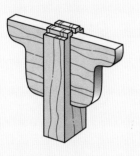

Edge Lap

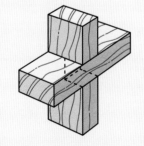

Double Lap

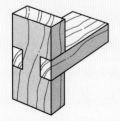

Cross- Lap

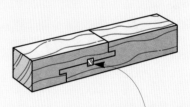

VARIATIONS

Mitered

Mitered and Chamfered

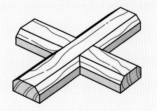

Triple Lap

Scarf Lap

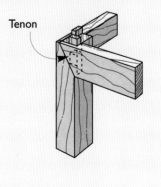

Optional tapered
pin locks joint.

Mitered Lap with Small Tenon

Tenon

Lap Joints

Lap joints are commonly used in frame construction, at the corners or in the middle of work where two or more members intersect. Typical examples are door and case frames, but there are so many varieties of lap joints that their usage is practically endless. One benefit is the ability to shape the joint after assembly, which allows you to introduce curves and other variations into your work.

Laps joints are some of the simplest joints to construct, since they usually consist of a flat cheek cut halfway through the thickness of a board. A small shoulder registers against the adjoining member, making fitting the joint relatively easy. (See Checking the Fit of a Lap, page 95.) The shoulder provides some resistance to racking, and the large overall surface area of the joint provides ample long-grain to long-grain gluing surfaces. However, wide frame members (more than 3 inches or so) can experience excessive wood movement, causing boards to expand and contract, which risks breaking the glue line. And there is a tendency for the joint to twist, especially joints that don't have some form of mechanical connection. The best approach is to keep frame members narrow, and to reinforce the joint with screws or pins. (See Reinforcing a Lap Joint, page 97.)

The table saw is king when it comes to constructing to lap joints—especially the more complex varieties. But don't overlook the router and the bandsaw when it comes to making this type of joint.

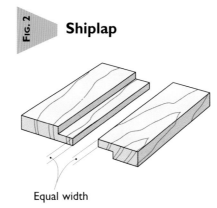

FIG. 2 **Shiplap**

Equal width

Shiplap

This is a good joint to choose when you need to make a wide panel from smaller boards. Compared to a regular butt joint (see page 43), a shiplap has more gluing area and the shoulders of the joint help significantly with alignment during assembly.

The key to a good shiplap—as with most lap joints—is to ensure that adjoining parts, such as the mating tongue and rabbet, are of equal thickness. This way, the joint will fit well and the two boards will come together flush during assembly. Another thing to keep in mind is to allow for some extra width when dimensioning your stock, to account for the material removed by the rabbet. This way, two joined boards will have the same width on their show faces. You can cut a shiplap on the table saw or on the router table.

On the table saw. Think of a shiplap as a pair of opposing rabbets that nest together, and you'll get an idea of how to construct the joint. You can use a standard blade, or a dado blade stacked to the desired width of the lap. With a single blade, you'll need to make each lap or rabbet in two cuts, first running the stock flat on the saw table and against the rip fence to rip a groove

equal to the depth of the rabbet. Then stand the stock upright against the fence and make a second pass, this time ripping the finished length of the rabbet. You'll remove a strip of wood in this second pass. Be sure to reorient the second mating piece so the rabbet opposes the rabbet in the first piece.

Cutting a shiplap with a dado blade is easier, because you make the cut in one pass and cut the mating piece without having to reset the blade height or the position of the rip fence. Set the blade height to the finished rabbet depth, and adjust the fence so the blade almost touches it, or attach a scrap board to the fence and bury the blade into it. Run your stock with opposite faces down on the saw, so the resulting laps will nest correctly.

On the router table. Routing a shiplap is similar to cutting the joint on the table saw, except you use a straight bit to cut the rabbets. For the smoothest cut, use the biggest diameter bit in

Corner cut. Set the bit height to the depth of the rabbet, and move the workpiece at an even feed speed. Pressure from a featherboard ensures the rabbet is of a consistent depth.

your collection. For really wide shiplaps, you could substitute a straight with a slot cutter. Adjust bit height to equal the depth of the rabbet, and position the fence to expose the correct amount of bit for the desired depth of the rabbet. Don't forget to position opposite faces of the stock on the table to ensure that matching faces will nest together when the joint is assembled. For the same reason, when joining three or more boards, cut rabbets on opposing sides of the same board, as shown in the bottom photo, opposite page.

Center lap. A dado blade makes quick work of cutting the center lap. The last pass is made against a stop block for accuracy.

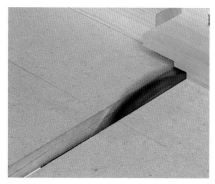

End lap. Without changing the blade height, cut the lap at the end of the mating piece. Make sure the stop block is tall enough to contact the uncut portion of the stock.

FIG. 3 ## Half-Lap

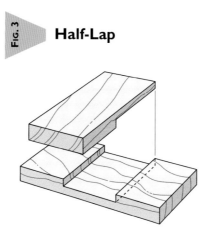

Half-Lap

Probably the most common of all lap joints, the basic half-lap is similar to a full lap joint, but because the mating pieces are shouldered, the joint is a bit stronger. You'll use this joint primarily for framework, where two frame members meet on the same plane and one butts into the middle of the other piece, or is inset from its end. You can use the table saw or the router table to make the joint. The bandsaw is useful for cutting the end-lap part of the joint.

On the table saw. The first half of the joint, where the lap is made across the center of the stock, is best cut on the double-runner sled (see page 21). You can use a standard saw blade for this cut, making repeated passes, but a dado blade is faster when you have multiple parts to cut. Set the blade height equal to the finished depth of the lap, or half of the stock's thickness (remember to take into account the sled's base), and use a stop block clamped to the sled's fence to help align the cut. (See middle left photo, above.)

You have a few options when it comes to cutting the lap on the end of the adjoining workpiece. The first approach is to use the same setup as you did for cutting the center lap, using the

Stand it up. Use the tenoning jig and a standard saw blade to make the cheek cut by orienting the stock perpendicular to the blade.

Lay it down. Adjust the blade to the depth of the lap and make the shoulder cut using the miter gauge. A long piece of plywood supports the work and lets you attach a stop block.

double-runner sled. Leave the blade height as is, and clamp a thicker stop block (it should contact the upper half of the stock's thickness) to the sled's fence to position the work for the cut, as shown in the photo, left.

If you don't want to bother setting up (or don't own) a dado blade, you can use the tenoning jig (see page 23). Clamp the stock vertically in the jig and set the rip fence to cut exactly one-half of the stock's thickness. Adjust the blade to make a full depth cut in one pass, then push the assembly past the blade. (See top photo, above.) Use the

Rout one shoulder. Push the stock over the bit using the sliding fence, starting at the far shoulder. A stop block prevents the bit from grabbing the workpiece and accurately locates the cut.

Complete the cut. Make the last pass by aligning the bit with the opposite shoulder, again using a stop block.

Rout the end. Move the stop block to rout the end lap, starting at the end of the work and finishing up by making a full pass at the shoulder line.

Fence and stop block. Use a fence and feed the work on edge and into the blade. A block clamped to the far end of the table stops the cut at the shoulder.

miter gauge to crosscut the waste and define the shoulder, adjusting the blade height equal to the depth of the lap. Attach a piece of plywood to the miter gauge fence so you can clamp a stop block to the plywood to guide the correct lap length. (See middle right photo, previous page.)

On the router table. Lay out and mark the joint on your stock. Then use the sliding fence (see page 29) and a large diameter straight bit to rout the joint. Adjust the bit height to the desired depth of the lap, and clamp a stop block at one end of the fence. Cut the center lap in successive passes, starting at one of your shoulder layout lines. Be sure to hold the stock against the stop block, as shown in the top photo, left. This will prevent the stock being thrown by the bit. Move the stop block with each pass, making the final pass with the bit lined up with the opposite shoulder. (See photo, far left.)

Use the same setup to rout the end lap, adjusting the stop block with each pass and making the final pass at the shoulder line. (See photo, left.)

On the bandsaw. The bandsaw is very effective for initial cutting of the end lap. Clamp a fence to the table (see Bandsaw/Drill Press Fence, page 25), adjusting the fence the correct distance from the blade so you cut one-half of the lap. Then clamp a stop block beyond the blade to limit the desired length of the lap. Push with an even feed speed through the blade, making sure the stock is firmly against the fence. (See photo, left.) Finish up by crosscutting the waste to the shoulder line with the miter gauge as you would using the table saw method described above.

Checking the Fit of a Lap

IT MAKES SENSE to check the fit of a trial joint before committing to the actual workpiece. Lap joints are especially important to check, since a good fit now will save headaches later. Set up your machines to make the cuts, then cut both halves of the joint and dry assemble it by hand, as shown in the photo. Check to see that the parts fit well and the surfaces of the joint are flush with each other. Then go ahead and cut the real thing.

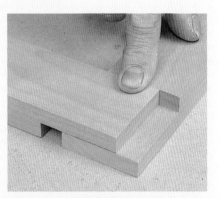

Accurate check. Press both halves of the joint together and feel with your finger to see that the surfaces are flush with each other.

FIG. 5

Corner Lap

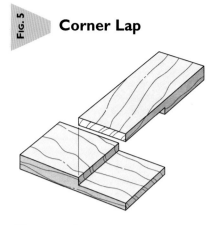

Corner Lap

A variation of the half-lap, the corner lap is a good choice for frames, such as door or picture frames. The nice thing about cutting a corner lap is that, once you've set up for the cut, both pieces can be machined without changing fence positions or cutter heights. This greatly simplifies your machine setup and speeds up the joint-cutting process. You can cut the joint on the table saw, on the router table, or on the bandsaw.

On the table saw. The joint is made in the same fashion as when constructing one-half of a half-lap (see page 93) using the double-runner sled and a dado blade, or with the tenoning jig.

On the router table. Install a large-diameter straight bit in the router and employ the sliding fence, using the same routing technique as when constructing one-half of a half-lap joint (see page 93).

On the bandsaw. Cut the cheeks of this joint using a fence and the same technique used when cutting one-half of a half-lap (see page 93). Once you've sawn the cheeks, remove the waste using the table saw approach as described when cutting a half-lap.

Full Lap

The full lap is a simple frame joint, and is widely used in furniture, cabinet, and construction work wherever an offset connection is needed. It's one of the simplest lap joints to construct, since you only need to machine one of the mating pieces; the second piece fits directly into the machined half of the joint.

Generally, the piece being machined should be twice as thick as the mating piece to ensure there's enough supporting material when the joint is assembled. Aim for a slightly tight fit when cutting the lap. This way, you can plane or sand the edges of the adjoining piece until the piece fits easily into the lap. You can construct this joint on the table saw or the router table.

FIG. 4

Full Lap

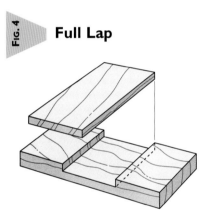

On the table saw. Cutting a full lap is best done with a dado blade, although you could certainly use a standard blade to nibble away the waste by making repeated passes. Use the double-runner sled to guide the work, using the same technique as when cutting a half-lap (see page 93).

On the router table. Install a large-diameter straight bit in the router, and use the sliding fence to rout the recess. The technique is identical to routing a half-lap (see page 93).

FIG. 6

Mitered-Corner Lap

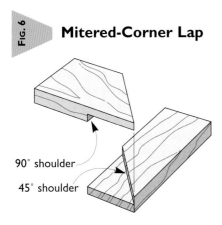

90° shoulder

45° shoulder

Mitered-Corner Lap

The mitered corner lap is a strong and elegant joint, and is a good choice for frames on which you want to show off the mitered detail. Although the joint looks complex, it is very simple to construct if you follow the correct machining sequence. Although you can cut the straight portion of the laps on the bandsaw or the router table (see Half-Lap, page 93), it's easier to set up and cut the entire joint on the table saw.

Nibbling away. Make successive passes with a standard saw blade to cut the end lap with a 90° shoulder. You won't need a stop block if you cut the joint overlong.

On the table saw. I like to use a standard saw blade for all the cuts, which simplifies setup. Although they appear to look alike, if you study the two halves of this joint you'll realize they have differing shoulders. One member has a shoulder at 90°; the opposite shoulder angles at 45°. Start by cutting the piece with the square shoulder. Using the single-runner sled (see page 20), adjust the blade height equal to the depth of the lap. Then cut the lap in successive passes by making nibbling cuts. You can make the lap overlong at this point, since a subsequent step will bring the lap to final length. (See bottom left photo, below.)

With the blade still set at the depth of the lap, cut the lap on the adjoining piece with its angled shoulder. As before, you can work with extra-long stock, and make the lap overlong. To make the lap cut, attach a 45° fence to the sled and cut the shoulder by holding the stock against the fence, making repeated passes over the blade. (See top photo, right)

Once you've cut the laps on both pieces, raise the blade and use the sled to cut the miter on the first piece, cutting it to finished length at the same time. You won't need a stop block to make this cut accurately. Just line up the previously cut shoulder with the edge of the blade's teeth or the edge of the jig, and hold the stock against the angled fence as you push the sled past the blade. (See middle photo, right.)

Now use the sled's 90° fence to cut the end of the second member to finished length. Again, simply line up the shoulder with the edge of the jig to make the cut, as shown in the photo, right.

Angled shoulder. Keep the blade at the same height and use a 45° fence to cut the angled shoulder, again cutting the lap longer than necessary and taking nibbling cuts.

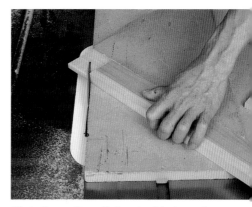

Cut the miter. Raise the blade and line up the shoulder with the edge of the jig to make the miter cut.

Square the end. Position the stock against the sled's rear fence to crosscut the end square, again lining up the shoulder with the edge of the jig.

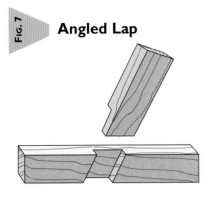

FIG. 7 **Angled Lap**

Angled Lap

In furniture construction, sometimes a joint is not at a 90° angle. The best example is a frame-type chair, where the framework, especially the seat frame, often comes together at a variety of angles. Or perhaps you need to join a custom frame for a door or picture at an unusual angle. The angled lap is a good choice for these types of projects, since it's relatively easy to make and helps maintain the strength of the structure you're building.

Luckily, constructing an angled lap joint is very simple. You can use the table saw to cut the joint, but make sure to lay out and mark the parts carefully and accurately before cutting.

On the table saw. Use the double-runner sled and the same cutting technique for making a half-lap (see page 93), except you install an angled fence onto the sled's base. Make the fence's angle equal to the angle you need for the joint, then position the stock on the sled and against the fence, and cut the half-laps in both pieces.

Another option is to cut the second part of the joint—the end lap—using the tenoning jig to make the cheek cut, and again using the same method as when cutting a half-lap (see page 93). Here, you'll need to angle

Reinforcing a Lap Joint

YOU NEED to reinforce many lap joints, especially those that have no mechanical connection, such as a half-lap, full lap, corner lap, or even a cross-lap joint. Generally, it's best to add reinforcement after you've glued, clamped, and assembled the joint. Figure 8 shows several options when it comes to choosing your strengthening method, from wooden pegs and dowels to screws, nails, or metal rods. Keep in mind that a pegged joint not only strengthens the lapped connection, but adds a decorative detail too.

FIG. 8 **Pinning the Joint**

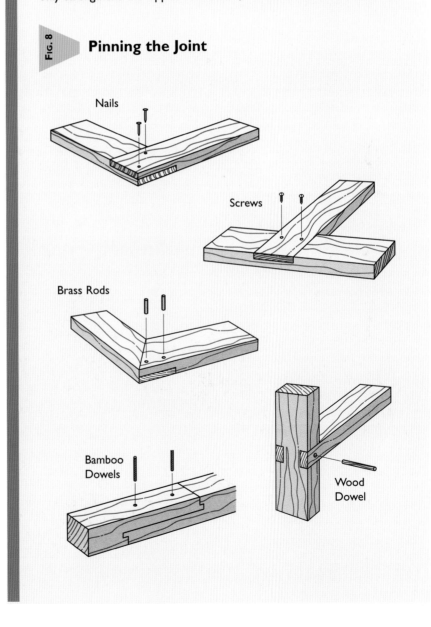

Nails

Screws

Brass Rods

Bamboo Dowels

Wood Dowel

the jig's stock support or clamp an angled fence to the jig to accommodate the desired angle of the joint. Once the cheek is cut, use the miter gauge set to the correct angle to crosscut the shoulder, using the same setup as when cutting a half-lap (see page 93).

Half-Blind Lap

The half-blind lap joint conveniently hides the end grain area of the end-lapped piece in a pocket cut inside the adjoining member, yet the joint is as strong as a regular half-lap joint. This feature is useful for frames in which one frame member butts into another, such as on a cabinet frame, and where you don't want the end grain to show. You can cut the joint using a combination of machines. The end lap can be made on the table saw, the router table, or the bandsaw, while the pocket is best cut on the router table or with a hand-held router.

On the table saw. Cut the first half of the joint—the lap at the end of the one frame piece—using one of the two methods used for cutting a half-lap (see page 93). You can either use a dado blade and the double-runner sled to cut the lap, or saw the cheek with a single blade and the tenoning jig. Finish by crosscutting to the shoulder line with the miter gauge. To cut the mating pocket for the lap, use the router table or a hand-held router.

On the router table. To rout the end lap, install a straight bit in the router, adjusting it to the desired depth of the lap. Use the sliding fence to guide the workpiece, following the same procedure as for cutting a half-lap (see page 93). To rout the matching pocket in the second piece, leave the bit height

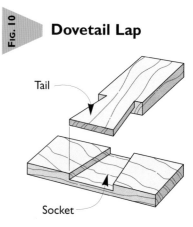

FIG. 9

Half-Blind Lap

as it is, and again use the sliding fence to guide the work over the bit. Here, you'll need to clamp a stop block to the router table top to limit the cut to the correct pocket length.

On the bandsaw. Cut the end lap using the same technique as for cutting a half-lap (see page 93). Then cut the pocket in the second piece on the router table or with a hand-held router.

With a hand-held router. While it's possible to cut the end lap with a hand-held router, I recommend using the table saw or the router table, since the setup is somewhat complicated. However, routing the pocket is simpler. Use the same approach as when routing a stopped dado (see page 84), using a straight bit and registering the workpiece and the router against the dado jig. Be sure to clamp the work securely to the bench, and secure a stop block to the bench or on the side of the dado jig to limit the length of the routed pocket.

Big tilt. Bevel the saw blade to the desired dovetail angle and cut each side of the tail in a single pass, holding the stock vertically in the tenoning jig.

FIG. 10

Dovetail Lap

Tail

Socket

Dovetail Lap

For a mechanically sound joint, try your hand at a dovetail lap joint. The wedging action of the dovetail makes the joint lock together, and makes it hard to pull the joint apart from one side. You can use this joint as a strong and decorative detail for all sorts of frames, or wherever you need additional strength. You can saw the tail member of the joint on the bandsaw, or make the entire joint on the table saw.

Cut the shoulders. Use a stop block and the single-runner sled to crosscut the waste and create the shoulders.

Lay out the socket. Use the tail to help with laying out the exact location of the socket.

On the table saw. Begin with the tail piece, laying out the desired dovetail angle on the stock. (For more on dovetail angles, see Useful Dovetail Angles, page 139.) Tilt the saw blade to your chosen angle and adjust its height to the length of the tail, then use the tenoning jig (see page 23) to rip the angle on both sides of the stock. (See bottom photo, opposite page.) Next, use the single-runner sled (see page 20) to crosscut the shoulder. A block clamped well forward of the blade will help you set the stock for the correct length, as shown in the photo, above. Clean up the inside corners of the tail with a few cuts from a sharp chisel. To complete the tail piece, make a lap cut on one side of the tail, using the tenoning jig or the double-runner sled and the same machine technique used for making a standard half-lap joint (see page 93).

Now use the sawn and lapped tail to lay out the sloped side of the dovetail socket. Place the shoulder of the tail piece against the socket stock and follow its outline with a pencil, as shown in the top right photo, above. Use a small square to square the sloped lines around to the edge of the stock.

To cut the socket, attach an angled fence, equal to the combined angle of the dovetail, to the double-runner sled. Using a standard saw blade, hold the stock against the fence and line up your square marks with the edge of the blade. Push the stock and sled through the blade to make the first shoulder cut, then make repeated passes to waste as much of the socket as possible. (See photo, left.) Be careful not to cut too far, or you'll saw past the smaller opening at the opposite edge of the piece. Finish the socket by turning the stock edge-for-edge and using the opposite side of the fence to cut the opposite sloped shoulder and remove the remaining waste, as shown in the photo, below.

Plow the socket. Place the work against an angled fence to cut the socket, registering the first cut against one side of the fence.

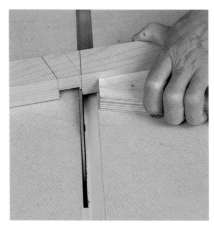

Finish from the other side. Cut the opposing shoulder with the stock against the opposite side of the fence.

Automatic angle. Push the workpiece and the angled jig as one unit into the blade to cut the sloping side of the tail.

On the bandsaw. You can make a very accurate tail cut on the bandsaw if you use a few jigs to help guide the cut. Start by clamping a straightedge to the saw table, a few inches away from the blade and square to the front edge of the table. Clamp a second block to the table behind the blade, such that it stops the cut at the desired tail length.

Now use an angled block, cut to the same angle as the desired slope of the dovetail, to guide the workpiece into the blade. A small scrap strip of wood nailed to the leading end of the block helps position the work accurately. (See photo, above.) To cut one sloping side in the workpiece, simply hold the work against the edge of the angled block and push the assembly into the blade until the block reaches the stop block. Repeat this procedure to saw the opposite slope. Finish the tail piece by making the lap cut on the table saw, using the same machine technique as for making a standard half-lap joint (see page 93).

Keyed-Dovetail Lap

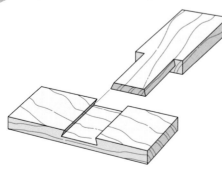

Keyed-Dovetail Lap

Similar to the dovetail lap, a keyed-dovetail lap joint prevents the parts from pulling apart—but from the opposite plane. The joint is appropriate for frames, and can be assembled without glue and secured with pins (see Reinforcing a Lap Joint, page 97), making it useful when you need to build frames that need to be knocked down or taken apart later. You can cut the joint on the table saw, or saw one-half of the joint on the bandsaw.

On the table saw. You'll cut the tail first. Start by ripping a scrap block to the desired slope of the dovetail. Save one of the offcuts from this block for a later step. Clamp the angled block to the tenoning jig (see page 23), adjust the blade height to the length of the tail, then hold the tail stock against the block to make the angled cheek cuts. Adjust the rip fence so the saw blade enters or exits at the very corner, or arris, of the work, depending on the side of the stock being sawn. (See photo, below.)

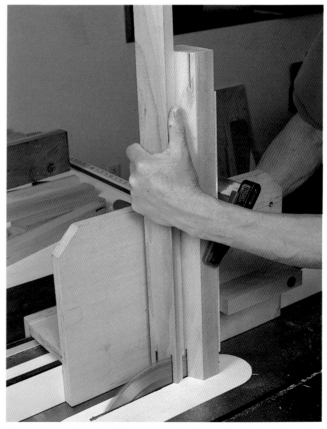

Saw at an angle. Cut the angled cheeks by holding the stock against an angled block clamped to the tenoning jig.

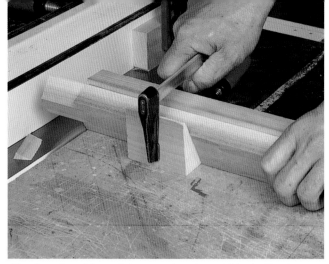

Sloping shoulders. A long wedge-shaped block tilts the work to the correct dovetail angle for crosscutting the shoulders. A second smaller blocks gives purchase for the clamp.

Stop and go. Place the work flat on the sled to make the lap cut, registering the work against the same stop-block setup used for the shoulder cuts.

Place the single-runner sled (see page 20) on the saw table, and use the leftover block you saved earlier (it should have the desired dovetail angle) to support the workpiece at the correct angle in the sled. Adjust the blade height to half of the stock's thickness, and make the shoulder cuts. A stop block clamped to the rip fence registers the shoulder cut, as shown in the photo, above. Leave the stop block on the rip fence, and reset the blade height to remove the waste on one side of the stock, making repeated passes with the blade. (See top right photo, above.)

Use the completed tail to lay out the location and angle for the socket, as shown in the photo, below. Now adjust the tilt of the saw blade to the angle of the dovetail, and use the single-runner sled to saw the socket, sawing one side of the socket and then turning the stock around to complete the opposite half. (See photo, below.) Use a chisel to clean up the corners of the socket.

On the bandsaw. The bandsaw is a good choice for making the cheek cuts on the tail, since this is a rip cut and the bandsaw easily powers its way through the cut. Start by laying out the shoulder line on the tail stock. While you could angle the saw table to make the cut, many bandsaw tables either tilt in only one direction, or they won't tilt far enough to provide the angle needed for dovetails. It's easier and more accurate to tilt the workpiece instead.

Use the same angled block you used for the table saw operation (see above), except that you nail a straight strip of wood to the angled face of the block. Lightly clamp a low fence to the table, then place the stock on the angled block

Trace the tail. Lay out the socket by positioning the completed tail against the edge of the work.

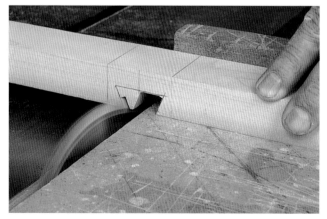

Tilt and saw. Make the two shoulder cuts with the blade tilted to the dovetail angle, moving the workpiece on the single-runner sled.

Saw one side. Rip the first side by placing the stock on an angled block and guiding the assembly against a low fence clamped to the table.

Saw the second side. Cut the opposite edge with the assembly turned end-for-end.

and adjust the fence until the blade lines up with one corner, or arris, of the tail stock. Tighten the clamps, and push the stock into the blade, stopping when you reach the shoulder line. (See top photo, above.)

Turn the block around (with the stock still against its fence) and readjust the fence to make the second cut. Push the stock into the blade as before, stopping when the work reaches the shoulder line. (See photo, above.) Remove the waste on the table saw as described above.

Bridle Joint

The bridle joint is one of the strongest types of lap joints, and more closely resembles a mortise-and-tenon joint in its nature. It's a good rail joint wherever you need to join an intersecting frame member in the middle of another. In general, it's best to proportion the joint such that each cheek of the notched piece is about one-third the total thickness of the material being joined. This way, both parts of the joint will have sufficient strength. The joint is probably best made entirely on the table saw, but you can use the router table to make the lap cuts and the bandsaw to saw the notch.

On the table saw. Make the lap cuts in the first half of the joint using the same technique as for constructing a half-lap (see page 93), running the stock on the double-runner sled and making the cuts with a standard saw blade or a dado blade. Remember to make lap cuts on both sides of the stock, leaving about one-third of the total material thickness in the center.

Fit the second half of the joint by cutting a notch in the adjoining piece. Again, use the same approach as when cutting a half-lap, holding the stock vertically to the blade with the tenoning jig. The difference here is that you make two cheek cuts, making sure to set the rip fence so the width of the notch equals the thickness of the material left in the first piece. Once you've cut the cheeks, remove the waste in the middle by resetting the rip fence and running the stock past the blade.

Fig. 12

Bridle Joint

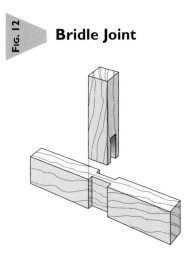

On the router table. Cutting the notch on the router table is impractical, since most bridle joints require a relatively deep notch that would need an extra-long router bit. But the lap cuts are simple to cut, and can be done with the same approach as cutting a half-lap (see page 93), using the sliding fence and a straight bit. Be sure to cut laps on both sides of the stock, then use the table saw or the bandsaw to cut the notches in the adjoining piece.

On the bandsaw. Cutting the notch is a simple affair on the bandsaw. Follow the same method used for cutting a half-lap (see page 93), using the fence to guide the stock into the blade. Make sure to set the fence so the blade cuts the two cheeks, then remove the waste in the middle by freehanding the stock into the blade. Finish up by cleaning up the bottom of the notch with a chisel.

Edge-Lap

The edge-lap joint is good for slender framework, such as a shoji-style screen, or when making inserts or dividers for small boxes, such as keepsakes and jewelry boxes. Since the joint doesn't have shoulders, it can twist and crack or break where the two halves intersect. That's why it's best to reserve this joint for small work, where little stress will be placed on the joined members.

Because the cut is the same on both workpieces, machine setup is simple. You can make the joint on the table saw, router table, or bandsaw.

On the table saw. Use the double-runner sled (see page 21) and either a standard saw blade or a dado blade for cutting this joint. If you install a dado blade that's the same width as the thickness of stock you're cutting, you can cut both parts of the joint in one pass. First set the blade height to half the width of your stock, then gang up mating workpieces and cut both notches at the same time. For accuracy, register the ends of the workpiece against a stop block clamped to the sled. (See photo, right.)

On the router table. Use the same method as when cutting a half-lap (see page 93), chucking a straight bit in the router and moving the workpiece past the bit with the sliding fence. The difference here is that you stand the stock on edge instead of on its face. If the required notches are deep, use a long bit and be sure take several passes by making successively deeper cuts with each pass until you reach a notch depth equal to half the width of the stock.

On the bandsaw. The best approach on the bandsaw is to lay out the joint and then freehand the cut by eye to your layout lines. Use a narrow blade, and make the shoulder cuts first. Then make a series of closely spaced interior cuts to remove the waste. Finish by sawing the bottom of each notch square to the shoulders.

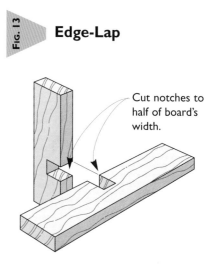

FIG. 13

Edge-Lap

Cut notches to half of board's width.

Two cuts in one. With the blade set to the exact thickness and one-half the width of the stock, hold both workpieces together to cut the joint in one pass.

Cutting a Long and Deep Lap

THIS IS AN interesting joint that's a variation on the standard bridle joint. The wide rail allows for a much deeper and stronger connection, acting as a brace and also as a decorative element. Used mostly as a rail joint, it's a good choice for joining a wide rail to a center table leg. The top of the leg has a pair of tenons that fits into matching mortises (not shown) in the underside of a tabletop.

The entire joint can be cut on the table saw. The first step is to saw the notch in the leg by raising the saw blade to full height and making successive passes on each side of the stock, moving the rip fence to cut each cheek and take away the waste between them. (See figure 14 and the top photos, right.) One warning: With the blade exposed in this manner, you must be extra careful; use a blade guard if possible. The next step is to cut the two tenons on the top of the leg, although these can be formed before cutting the notch if you prefer. (For more on multiple tenons, see page 113.)

Lay out the curves on the rail stock, but before cutting out the profile, make the two lap cuts using the same procedure as when making a standard half-lap (see page 93). Next, make a relief cut on its bottom edge to allow for the curvature at the bottom of the leg notch. You can make this cut by standing the stock vertically on the double-runner sled, as shown in the bottom photo, right. Once the joinery is complete, saw the profile on the rail by following your layout lines on the bandsaw, then clean up the saw marks with a scraper or a drum sander. Finish up by rounding over the leg using a hand plane or a roundover bit in the router table.

 Fig. 14

Cutting a Long and Deep Lap

1. Cut notch on table saw with blade raised full height, cutting from both sides of stock. (See top photos.)

2. Cut tenons at top of leg.

3. Cut laps in rail to fit notch in post. (See bottom photo.)

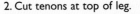

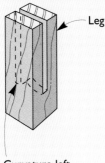

Leg

Curvature left by blade's radius

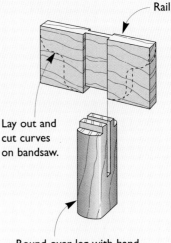

Rail

Lay out and cut curves on bandsaw.

Round over leg with hand plane or router bit.

Long notch. With the blade raised to full height, make a series of cuts from both sides of the stock (top), stopping each cut when the end of the work contacts the stop block (above).

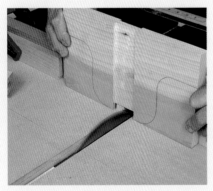

Cut some relief. Notch the bottom of the rail to allow for the curve in the bottom of the leg notch. A stop block ensures accurate shoulders.

FIG. 15 **Double-Lap**

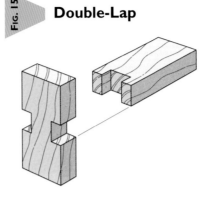

Double-Lap

The double-lap joint is used in furniture, cabinet, and building construction and is a strong joint because of its interlocking elements. Further reinforcement with pins can significantly increase its overall strength (see Reinforcing a Lap Joint, page 97). Construction is almost identical to the edge-lap joint, and can be done on the table saw, router table, or bandsaw.

On the table saw. Use the same approach as when cutting an edge-lap (see page 103), using either a standard saw blade or a dado blade and the double-runner sled. The difference here is that you'll need to cut adjoining parts separately. Start by cutting the two outer notches on the first piece. Adjust the blade height equal to the thickness of the adjoining stock, and position the stock on edge for the first notch. Then flip the stock over and cut the second notch in the same manner. Once you've notched the first piece, lay out and cut the mating center notch in the second piece with the blade at the same height by standing the stock on its end.

On the router table. Use the same technique as when cutting a half-lap (see page 93), chucking a straight bit in the router and moving the workpieces past the bit with the sliding fence. Rout the two outer notches first, standing the stock on the opposite edge to make the cuts. Then rout the mating center notch in the second piece by standing the stock vertically against the fence.

On the bandsaw. Cut the two outer notches as you would when cutting an edge-lap (see page 103), laying out the joint and cutting to your lines by eye. Then use the same approach as when cutting a half-lap (see page 93), registering the workpiece against a fence. Finish up by squaring the bottom of the notch with a chisel.

FIG. 16

Cross-Lap

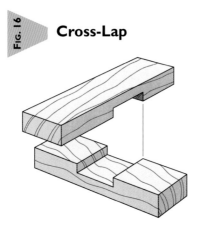

VARIATIONS

Mitered

Miter shoulders
where laps intersect.

Mitered-and-Chamfered

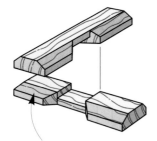

Cut mitered cross-lap,
then chamfer edges.

Cross-Lap

The cross-lap, and its decorative variations—the mitered cross-lap and the mitered-and-chamfered cross-lap—is used extensively in furniture construction, particularly in medium to small framework, such as door mullions or shoji-type screens. With the more decorative versions, not only is the construction structure important, but the joinery itself can become part of the design and shows quality craftsmanship.

The three types of cross-lap joints shown are all basically the same joint, but with different details. Both halves of the joint are identical, which makes machinery setup a simple affair, although the decorative versions require more steps. You can cut the basic joint on the table saw, the router table, or with a hand-held router. The table saw is the tool of choice for cutting the mitered cross-lap and the mitered-and-chamfered cross-lap.

On the table saw. For a standard cross-lap, use the same technique as when cutting a half-lap (see page 93), sawing the joint on the double-runner sled. You can use a standard saw blade by making repeated passes, but a dado blade is much faster, especially when cutting multiple parts.

For the mitered and mitered-and-chamfered cross-lap joints, good layout is the key to a good joint. Start by laying out the joint on the inside face of both halves, using the width of the stock to determine the outer edges of your layout. Draw 45° miter lines at these outside edges with a combination square, then draw square lines from the inside of the miters to define the lap areas, as shown in the top photo, above. Cut the laps in each

Layout is the key. A combination square helps with laying out the miters, which locate where to make the lap cut (shown by a series of diagonal lines drawn on the piece in the background).

Refine the lap. Make the shoulder cuts equal to the depth of the miters, holding the stock firmly against the sled's fence.

Miter the shoulders. Cut the miters by tilting the saw blade to 45° and aligning it with the shoulders. A clamp ensures accuracy for this critical cut.

piece using the same approach as above, being careful to stay within your inner layout lines.

Once you've cut the laps, raise the blade equal to the depth of the miters and make the shoulder cuts, then remove the waste between the shoulders by taking nibbling cuts. (See middle photo, opposite page.) Tilt the blade to 45° and cut the miters to finish up the mitered cross-lap, as shown in the bottom photo, opposite page.

To complete the mitered-and-chamfered cross-lap, tilt the saw blade and use the rip fence to cut chamfers on one face of each half. The specific bevel angle of the blade will depend on the thickness of your stock, but generally a chamfer of about 20° works well. Another option is to plane the chamfers by hand with a plane.

On the router table. Routing the cross-lap is identical to cutting a half-lap (see page 93) by using the sliding fence and a large-diameter straight bit. Once you've set the bit height to the desired depth of the lap, use a stop block at one end of the fence and cut the lap in each member in successive passes, starting at a shoulder.

With a hand-held router. Use the same procedure as when cutting a half-lap (see page 93), cutting the pocket in each piece with a straight bit and the dado jig.

Fig. 17

Triple-Lap

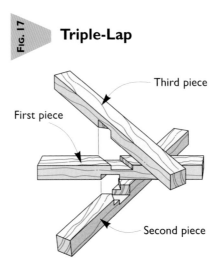

First piece
Third piece
Second piece

Triple-Lap

The triple-lap is a beautiful joint, typically seen in old Chinese furniture, and is used for framework where three members intersect. It looks complicated, but it's actually quite simple to make on the table saw using the double-runner sled (see page 21). Each member joins its neighbor at an angle of 60°, which simplifies setup and construction. One note: Be sure the three pieces of your stock are exactly the same width and thickness so the parts will fit precisely.

On the table saw. Start by laying out the joint on the three members, dividing the thickness of the stock into thirds.

You'll use a 60° fence attached to the base of the double-runner sled. With the work placed against one edge of the fence, you create an effective cutting angle of 60°. (For more on angled fences for the sled, see page 21.) Install a dado blade on the saw and adjust its height to one-third of the thickness of your stock. You can use a standard saw blade for these cuts, but a dado blade will make the operation much faster. Cut a lap in the first piece so its length equals the stock's width, holding the piece against the near side of the angled

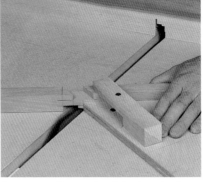

Lap one. Cut each of the laps in the first piece with the stock against the front, or near side, of the fence. A hold-down screwed to the sled's base keeps the stock secure during the cuts.

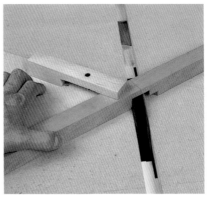

Lap two. Cut the lap in the second piece by making two cuts from each side of the fence. Raise the blade to two-thirds height for the second cut.

fence. Then flip the piece over and cut an opposing lap, registering the workpiece against the same fence edge. Align this second lap cut by squaring the shoulder line across the stock from the first lap, as shown in the top photo, above. Again, cut the lap length equal to the width of the stock.

Now make the two lap cuts in the second piece. Cut the first lap with the blade height as is, registering the workpiece from the far side of the angled fence. Then raise the blade height to equal two-thirds of the stock's thickness, and without flipping the stock over, place the piece against the near fence and cut the second lap. (See photo, above.)

Last lap. The third piece is cut twice with the blade remaining at two-thirds height. Make the first cut at the far side of the fence; the second cut is made with the stock against the near side.

Three's company. The completed joint tells the story, revealing the lap cuts from the first piece to the last, arranged here from left to right.

The last piece also receives two lap cuts, and both can be made without altering the blade height. Make the first cut with the piece against the far side of the fence. Then on the same face, cut the second lap by registering the piece against the near side of the fence, as shown in the top photo, above. The three finished pieces reveal the cutting procedure, and should fit together with light taps from a mallet. (See photo, above.)

 **Fig. 18**

Scarf Lap

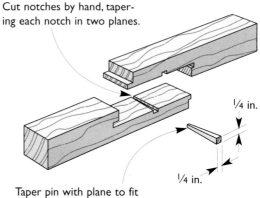

Cut notches by hand, tapering each notch in two planes.

Taper pin with plane to fit notch once joint is assembled.

¼ in.

¼ in.

Scarf Lap

In its simplest form, this joint is known as a scarf lap. Because of its mechanical connection, this is a great joint for connecting two pieces end-to-end by gluing the parts and clamping them until the glue dries. However, by adding a tapered pin that fits into a tapered notch cut in both halves, you can join the pieces without glue. This variation is known as a scarf lap with pin, or in Chinese as a "wedge-nail joint." The nail, or wooden pin, is wedge-shaped on all four faces, and effectively prevents the two pieces from coming apart, making glue optional. You'll find this joint in framework, and typically on continuous rails found on some Chinese furniture. The joint can be cut quite easily on the table saw, especially since the halves are identical.

On the table saw. For the joint to fit precisely, it's important that both pieces be accurately milled to the same thickness and width. Start by laying out the joint on your stock, dividing the thickness of each piece in half and drawing the long lap. I usually aim for a deep lap cut of around 3 inches—the limit of a standard saw blade. Use the tenoning jig (see page 23) to make the cheek cut on both pieces, aligning the rip fence so the edge of the cut is exactly centered on the stock's thickness. (See top left photo, opposite page.)

Next, cut the shoulder of each lap on the single-runner sled (see page 20), staying about $3/16$ inch away from the end

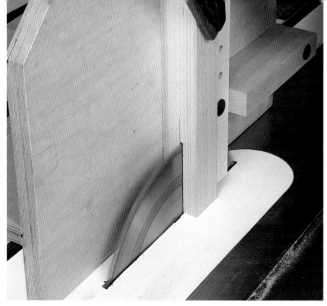

Deep rip. Raise the blade to full height and use the tenoning jig to make the cheek cut in the exact center of the stock.

Pinned tight. The joint can be locked together without glue by tapping a tapered pin into tapered notches cut in both halves.

Shy shoulder. Clamp a stop block to the rip fence to register the end of the workpiece, cutting the shoulder about 3/16 inch in from the cheek cut.

of the cheek cut, as shown in the photo, left. Then lower the blade 1/8 inch and nibble the end until you form a small tenon that fits into the notch left by the previous cut. (See bottom left photo, below.) The joint should fit together seamlessly, and adding a wooden pin will help to keep it tight without glue. (See photo, above.)

Form the tenon. Reset the fence with the stop block attached to cut the tenon, sawing its shoulder to the same depth as the notch.

FIG. 19

Mitered Lap with Small Tenon

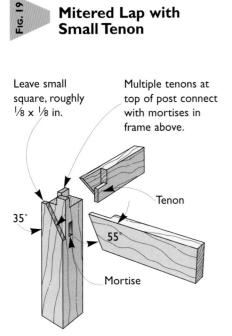

Leave small square, roughly ⅛ x ⅛ in.

Multiple tenons at top of post connect with mortises in frame above.

35°

55°

Tenon

Mortise

Mitered Lap with Small Tenon

This is a fairly complex joint that consists of lap as well as mortise-and-tenon joints. The joint is often seen in chair, table, and cabinet construction, or wherever a post meets two thinner yet wider rails that run 90° to each other. The resulting miter on each outer face combines with small mortises and tenons to not only make the joint very strong, but also very beautiful. Adjacent tenons at the top of the post fit into corresponding mortises cut into the undersides of a table apron or frame above the post (not shown). The lap-cutting procedures can be done on the table saw. For more on cutting the mortises and tenons, see page 113.

On the table saw. Start with the two rails, and use the tenoning jig (see page 23) to make the cheek cut that defines the lap on each piece, standing the stock vertically in the jig. Make the laps roughly one-third the thickness of the rails. Move the rip fence and make a second cut for the inside cheek of the small tenon, which should also be about one-third of the stock's thickness. Remove the waste between the two cuts by successive movements of the rip fence. Next, cut a 55° miter by laying the stock horizontally on the single-runner sled against a 110° fence attached to its base (see Table Saw Sleds, page 20). Adjust the blade height to cut the miter, but not high enough to cut into the tenon area. Finish the rails by laying out the small tenons, making them half the width of the stock, and sawing them out by hand.

Start with overlong stock for the post. You'll form the adjacent tenons at the top of the post after completing the lap joints. (For more on adjacent tenons, see page 126.) Use the same procedure as when cutting a mitered-corner lap (see page 96) to cut the adjacent 35° mitered laps in the post. Attach a 70° fence to the single-runner sled and make nibbling cuts with a standard blade, making the lap overlong to allow for subsequent machining of the tenons. Without changing the blade height, remove the angled fence and make a 90° cut on each outside face to create a small ⅛-inch flat at the top of the post. Keeping the top square in this manner prevents the sharp tips of the rail miters from extending all the way to the outside and causing possible damage, and makes a cleaner joint. Finish by cutting the adjacent tenons at the top of the post and cutting the mortises on the two inner faces.

FIG. I ◀ **MORTISE-AND-TENON JOINTS** (continued next page)

Slip Joint

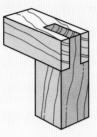

VARIATION
Multiple Tenons

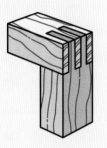

Mitered Slip Joint

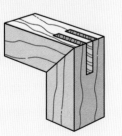

Basic Mortise-and-Tenon

No Shoulder

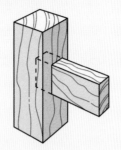

Shoulder Two Sides

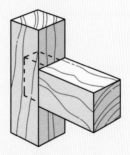

Shoulder Four Sides

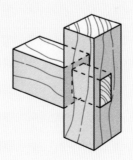

Haunched Tenons

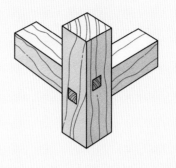

Haunched-Mitered Tenon

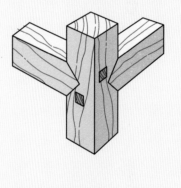

Adjacent Tenons

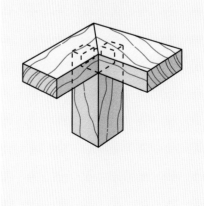

FIG. 1 ◄ **MORTISE-AND-TENON JOINTS** (continued)

Loose Tenon

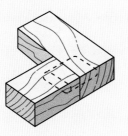

Through-Wedge Tenon

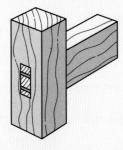

VARIATIONS

Multiple Tenons

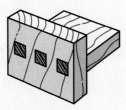

Round Stock

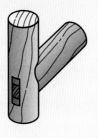

Angled Tenon

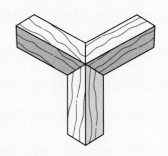

Mitered Corner with Through-Tenon

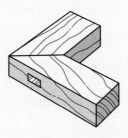

Double Miter

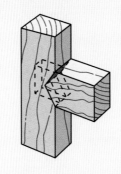

Three-Way Miter

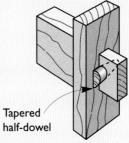

Knock-Down Mortise-and-Tenon

Doweled

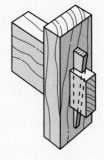

Tapered half-dowel

Wedged

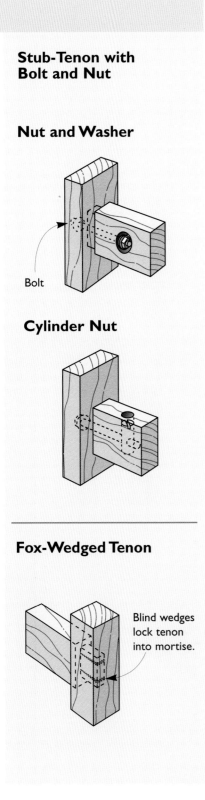

Stub-Tenon with Bolt and Nut

Nut and Washer

Bolt

Cylinder Nut

Fox-Wedged Tenon

Blind wedges lock tenon into mortise.

Mortise-and-Tenon Joints

The mortise-and-tenon is arguably the most basic of all joints in woodworking. The joint is one of the strongest methods for joining parts at angles to each other, especially where pieces meet at right angles. It's a very common joint in framework, cabinet and furniture construction, and even in wood buildings. Many variations of the mortise-and-tenon are often seen in traditional Chinese furniture. The mortise, a squared or rectangular recess cut in one workpiece (partway or all the way through), accepts the tenon, a tongue-shape on the end of the connecting piece. Although the connecting members join cross-grain to each other, by keeping the parts relatively narrow (under 3 inches or so) you won't have to worry about wood movement. A sliding fit between the tenon and the mortise—plus glue—keeps parts sound for a long time. And the joint readily accepts pegs or pins for further reinforcement (see Pegging a Mortise-and-Tenon Joint, page 131).

The good news is that you have many choices when it comes to cutting mortises and tenons. The table saw is particularly adept at sawing all sorts of tenons, especially when equipped with jigs. But other machines work just as well, including the router and the bandsaw. Cutting mortises can be done with the router, the mortising-and-tenoning fixture, or on the drill press. And one dedicated machine—the hollow-chisel mortiser—really shines when it comes to milling mortises.

Slip Joint

The simplest of all mortise-and-tenon joints, the slip joint—also called an open-tenon joint—is used extensively in framework, and it often becomes a decorative element thanks to its exposed joinery. The joint consists of a tenon that fits into an open notch, rather than a traditional enclosed mortise. You use the slip joint on the corners of frames; its cousin, the lap bridle joint (see page 102) takes care of connections made in the middle of frame pieces. Because there are no enclosed mortises to cut, making a slip joint is relatively simple and the machinery setup is fundamental.

A slip joint with multiple tenons is a variation on the basic joint. This is the joint to choose when you're working

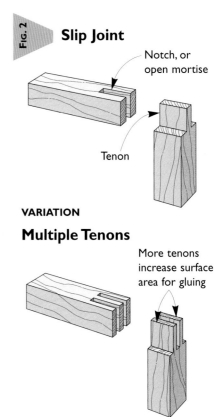

Fig. 2

Slip Joint

Notch, or open mortise

Tenon

VARIATION

Multiple Tenons

More tenons increase surface area for gluing

Tenon first. Cut the tenon cheeks with a single setup by flipping the stock 180° in the jig after the first cut.

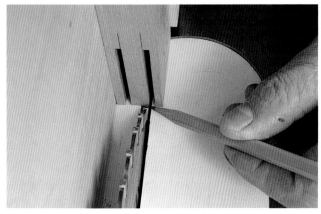

Simplified setting. Use the sawn tenon to align the jig for the notch cuts in the second piece, aligning a saw tooth with one edge of a cheek.

with very slender stock, such as a narrow door or case frame that needs to hold glass or other heavy panels. With its multiple tenons, the joint benefits from an increased gluing area, which significantly beefs up the joint's overall strength and provides resistance to racking. You can make slip joints on the table saw or bandsaw.

On the table saw. My favorite approach is to use the tenoning jig (see page 23) and a standard saw blade for cutting the tenon and the notch. Start by cutting the tenon first, clamping the stock vertically in the jig and making two successive cheek cuts, flipping the stock 180° after the first cut to rip the second cheek. (See photo, left.) For a precisely centered tenon, make sure to test your setup on scrap before cutting the real thing.

Without removing the stock from the tenoning jig, use this first piece to reset the jig for the notch cuts in the mating piece by lining up the blade with the inner edge of one of the cheek cuts, as shown in the middle photo, left. Use the same approach as before, making the first cheek cut in the notch stock, then reorienting the stock 180° in the jig to cut the second cheek. (See bottom left photo, below.) Remove the remaining waste between the cheek cuts by moving the rip fence (and the jig) closer to the blade, again cutting with one face against the jig and then flipping over the stock to make the cut from the opposite side. (See photo, below.)

Once you've cut both the tenon and the notch, the last step is to cut the shoulders on the tenon piece, which can be done while the stock is still in the jig or with the use of a sled. (See Cutting Shoulders on the Table Saw, page 122.)

Cutting a multiple-tenon slip joint involves the same setup, but with a few more steps. As before, cut the tenons first, then use them to help realign the jig for cutting the

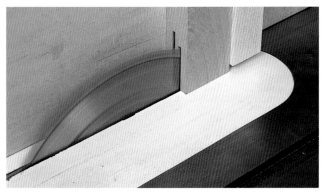

Notch second. Rip the cheeks of the notch as you did the tenon, turning the stock 180° for the second cut.

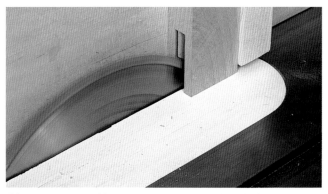

Rip the waste. Move the jig closer to the blade to remove the waste between the cheeks.

multiple notches. The main difference in cutting a multiple-tenon slip joint is that you must move the jig at least twice (depending on the thickness of your stock) after making the two initial cheeks cuts in order to define both sides of the tenons. (See photo, right.)

As before, use the tenon piece to align the jig for sawing the notches in the mating piece. First saw the cheeks, then readjust the rip fence to widen the notches. Again, take two successive cuts by flipping the stock 180° after the first cut, as shown in the middle photo, right.

On the bandsaw. Use a straightedge or the bandsaw/drill press fence (see page 25) clamped to the bandsaw table to accurately cut both the notch and the tenon. The setup is identical when sawing multiple tenons, although you'll have to either adjust the fence for multiple cuts, or clamp the fence further from the work and use shims of the correct thickness between the work and the fence. Make the cheek cuts in the tenon stock first, using a stop block clamped at the outfeed end of the table to regulate the correct tenon length. (See bottom photo, right.) Use the tenon to lay out the notch, readjust the fence, and repeat the cutting sequence to make the cheek cuts. Remove the waste by freehanding the work into the blade. If you're careful, you can get a clean cut at the bottom of the notch. If necessary you can square up this area with a chisel or a file.

Once the cheeks are cut, crosscut the shoulders on the tenon piece using the same procedure as when cutting a basic mortise-and-tenon (see page 117).

Two tenons. Cut the tenon cheeks by flipping the stock 180°, then move the jig sideways to cut the shoulders and remove the waste in the center.

Two notches. Rip the outer cheeks of the notches first, then move the jig sideways and saw the inner cheeks, again flipping the work 180° for the second cut.

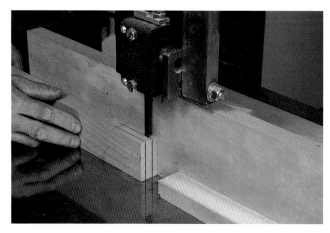

Bandsawing a tenon. Guide the work against the fence, making two cuts by turning the stock 180° for the second cut. A stop block controls the correct tenon length.

Cutting Two Cheeks in One Pass

USING THE tenoning jig (see page 23) is a wonderful method for ripping tenons on the table saw with a standard saw blade. But you can significantly speed up the process by installing two blades on the arbor instead of one. The technique allows you to rip two parallel cheeks in one pass, saving setup and machining time. This is an especially useful technique whenever you're faced with making lots of tenons.

If you own a dado blade, use the two outer blades for this operation. Alternatively, you can use any pair of matched blades, such as two identical 7 1/4-inch circular saw blades, as long as the two blades are exactly the same diameter. Bandsaw a plywood spacer about 3 inches in diameter, and drill a hole (typically 5/8 inch) through the center of the spacer to fit your saw's arbor. Make the spacer the same thickness as your desired tenon thickness. Install the first blade, slide the spacer over the arbor, and install the second blade up against the spacer. Tighten the assembly with the saw's washer and arbor nut. Now get ready to use the tenoning jig to cut perfect tenons without having to flip the stock after each pass.

Sawing double-time. Saw a tenon in one pass using the two outside chippers from the same dado set. A wooden shim installed on the arbor and between the blades regulates the precise tenon thickness.

FIG. 3 **Mitered Slip Joint**

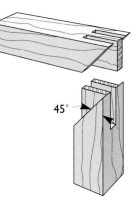

45°

Mitered Slip Joint

This joint is very similar to the multiple-tenon slip joint, except it has a mitered joint line, which adds a visual detail. This is another joint that works well for framework, and can provide a little variation in your woodwork without sacrificing strength and rigidity. The table saw is the tool of choice for making this joint.

On the table saw. Start with overlong stock; you'll trim it to final length later. Install the tenoning jig and use the same table saw approach as when cutting a multiple-tenon slip joint (see page 113). Be sure to cut a single, centered notch in the first piece, raising the blade a little higher than the finished tenon length. The second piece receives two similarly overlong notches, with its center tenon aligned with the notch in the first piece. (See photo, opposite page.)

Use the single-runner sled and a 45° fence to saw the shoulders. Using the same approach as when cutting a mitered-corner lap joint (see page 96), lay the stock flat on the sled and cut 45° shoulders on both sides of each piece, lining up the saw blade with the bottom of the notch cuts. Be sure to lower the saw blade so it doesn't cut into the tenon cheeks. You can cut each shoulder on the double-notched piece in one pass; make successive passes on each side of the single-notched member, taking nibbling cuts until you've formed the tenon cheek.

Saw the notches first. Use the tenoning jig to cut a single notch in the first piece. Then saw twin notches (above) in the adjoining member, aligning its center tenon with the notch in the first piece.

Finish up by cutting the pieces to finished length, raising the blade to cut through the stock. Crosscut each piece so the ends of the tenons meet right at the very tips of the long point of the mitered shoulders. Use the 90° fence on the single-runner sled for this operation, again employing the same approach as when cutting a mitered-corner lap joint.

Basic Mortise-and-Tenon

There are three variations on the basic mortise-and-tenon, with distinctions that relate to the tenon itself: a tenon without a shoulder; a tenon shouldered on two faces; and a tenon shouldered on all four faces. Your choice will depend on your design requirements and your specific needs. An unshouldered tenon, often referred to as a barefaced tenon, is simple to make, but should be used with discretion, since the lack of

 Basic Mortise-and Tenon

No Shoulder

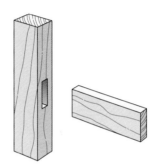

Shoulder Two Sides

Shoulders bear against post to prevent racking.

Shoulder Four Sides

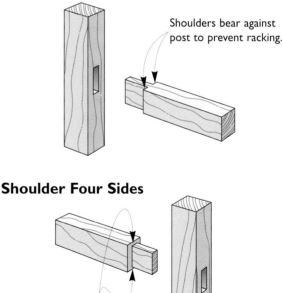

Small shoulders hide any blemishes above and below mortise.

shoulders reduces the joint's ability to resist racking. You can use this joint where members are too thin to allow for shoulders, and it's useful when you need many tenons to spread out a load, such as in the multiple slats of a chair. Also, not having to account for shoulders makes layout, dimensioning, and construction much simpler. Keep in mind that a tenon without shoulders won't offer the advantage of hiding blemishes, such as a sloppily cut mortise or dings around its mouth.

A tenon shouldered on two faces offers good resistance to racking, and only lacks the ability to hide blemishes on its two unshouldered sides. But its ease of layout often overcomes this small deficit, since your mortise length will correspond directly with the width of your tenon stock. For maximum support and good looks, a mortise-and-tenon with four shoulders offers the best choice.

The basic mortise-and-tenon can be cut using a combination of machines, from the table saw, bandsaw, and router to the hollow-chisel mortiser and drill press. Generally, it's best to mill the mortise first, then cut the tenon, since it's usually easier to adjust the final dimension of the tenon to get a perfect fit into the mortise.

On the table saw. Don't expect to mill mortises on the table saw—other machines do a better job of cutting these enclosed pockets, as I'll describe. But the table saw is a workhorse when it comes to milling tenons. There are two approaches you can take. The tenoning jig (see page 23) is the primary device for sawing tenons. Setup is the same as when cutting a slip joint (see page 113), standing the work vertically in the jig and ripping the tenon cheeks. Once the

cheeks are formed, cut the shoulders by moving the rip fence and the jig or lay the stock flat and crosscut the stock with a sled (see Cutting Shoulders on the Table Saw, page 122).

The second option for cutting the tenon is to use a dado blade and the double-runner sled. The technique is similar to cutting a half-lap (see page 93), except that you flip over the stock after cutting one cheek to mill the opposite side. This is a very effective way to cut a lot of tenons quickly and easily. You can cut the shoulders with the same blade and the same setup, adjusting the blade to the correct height and standing the workpiece on edge.

On the bandsaw. While the bandsaw does an excellent job of sawing slip joints (see page 113), it's not suitable for milling enclosed mortises. But sawing tenons is easy and safe on the bandsaw, especially with large or thick stock. Begin by cutting the cheeks, using a fence clamped to the table and following the same procedure as when cutting a slip joint (see page 115).

Without changing the fence setup, saw the tenon to width and form the small shoulders, inserting a shim between the fence and the work equal to the desired shoulder depth. (See top photo, right.)

Next, readjust the fence to the desired tenon length, and position the work perpendicular to the fence to remove the waste. Use a wide piece of scrap to help guide the workpiece and keep it from tipping away from the fence, as shown in the middle photo, right. Without moving the fence, position the stock on edge and saw the large shoulders, again using a backup block to guide the workpiece. (See photo, right.)

Saw to width. By slipping a shim between the fence and the workpiece, you can use the same fence setting used to rip the cheeks for sawing the tenon to width. A stop block limits the length of the cut.

Short shoulders. Set the fence to the tenon length and make the small shoulder cuts by guiding the work with a wide piece of scrap.

Long shoulders. With the same fence setup, saw the large shoulders with the workpiece on edge, resetting the stop block and again using the scrap to guide the cut.

Routing in steps. Use a wide piece of scrap to guide the work past the bit, starting at the end of the stock (top) and taking ¼-inch-wide cuts until the stock contacts the fence (above).

On the router table. The router table does a respectable job of routing tenons, especially if you equip it with a large-diameter straight bit. You'll need to look to another setup or machine for cutting mortises. To rout a tenon, begin by setting the bit height to the correct shoulder depth of the tenon, then adjust the fence away from the bit so that the distance from the fence to the outer edge of the bit equals the desired tenon length.

Use a wide piece of scrap to help guide the narrow workpiece past the bit, and start by routing the end of the workpiece with the stock away from the fence. Make the cheek cuts in ¼- to ½-inch increments, taking the final pass with the stock riding firmly against the fence, as shown in the photos, left. Once you've routed one side, flip the stock over and repeat to rout the opposite side. Cut the small shoulders by adjusting the bit to the correct height and standing the workpiece on edge. Again, use wide scrap to guide the cut.

With a hand-held router. While it's possible to mill tenons with a hand-held router, it's not particularly practical. But a plunge router equipped with a straight bit is the tool preferred by many small-shop woodworkers when it comes to routing mortises.

Setup is simple: Clamp the stock securely in a large bench vise with the edge of the work flush with the bench surface. Clamp a straightedge (a piece of straight plywood works great) parallel to and at the correct distance from the workpiece, such that the router bit is centered on the stock when the router's base engages the edge of the straightedge. Set the router's depth rod equal to the desired depth of the mortise. You can rout the mortise freehand, plunging in ⅛-inch increments and moving the router until you reach layout marks at each end of the mortise. For more security, try clamping stop blocks at each end of the mortise to control the length of the cut. (See photo, below.) When cutting mortises in the manner, remember to either round over the edges of the tenon with a file to fit the rounded ends of the mortise, or square up the mortise with a chisel.

With the mortising-and-tenoning fixture. Both the mortise and the tenon can be cut quickly and efficiently using this shop-made device (see page 31). Start by routing the mortise, laying out its length and orienting the stock parallel to the fence of the fixture. Adjust the length of the bit from the face of the fence to correspond to the desired mortise depth, and set its height so the bit is centered on the stock thickness. Clamp the stock firmly with the toggle clamps. Now push

Plunging mortises. Guide the router against a straightedge clamped to the bench, and rout in successive passes by taking ⅛-inch-deep cuts until you reach the bottom of the mortise.

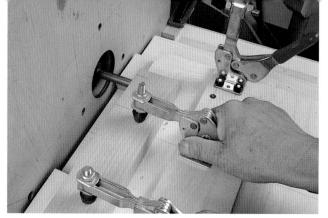

Mortising a slot. Move the work into the bit, taking ⅛-inch-deep cuts and moving the piece sideways to lengthen the mortise.

Trimming a tenon. Cut the tenon with the bit above the work, flipping the work 180° to rout the second face and again taking ⅛-inch cuts until the work contacts the fence.

Clean inside and out. The finished tenon is flat and clean, and the round-ended mortise has wonderfully smooth walls.

the stock into the spinning bit in ⅛-inch increments while moving it sideways, stopping at your layout marks, as shown in the photo, left. Continue in this manner until the stock contacts the fence.

Now cut the tenon. This time, orient the stock perpendicular to the jig's fence, and clamp it securely with the toggle clamps. Leave the bit length as is, but adjust the bit height so the workpiece will be cut from above and equal to the correct shoulder depth. Use the same routing procedure as before, taking ⅛-inch cuts and moving the stock sideways until the end of the workpiece contacts the fence. Then flip over the stock and repeat the cutting sequence on the opposite side, as shown in the middle photo, left.

The resulting tenon should have a very smooth face, and the full-depth mortise should be cleanly cut with rounded ends. (See bottom photo, left.) If you want, you can use the same fixture to rout the tenon shoulders by adjusting the bit height. However, it's usually more practical to make these cuts on another machine, such as the table saw. (See Cutting Shoulders on the Table Saw, page 122.)

The last step is to round over the edges of the tenon with a file, or square the ends of the mortise with a chisel.

With the hollow-chisel mortiser. For traditional square-ended mortises, this machine is a joy to use. Setup is straightforward: Lay out the mortise location on the edge of the stock, and mark a centerline as well. Clamp the stock in the machine's vise, and adjust the fence until the bit is centered on the stock. Start at each end of the mortise, plunging straight down and then pulling up to cut a square pocket, as shown in the top left photo, opposite page. Then remove the waste in the middle by moving the table and plunging in successive passes, taking a full-depth cut with each pass. (See middle photo, opposite page.) The finished mortise won't be as clean as a routed version, but the ends will be dead square and ready to receive a traditional square-sided tenon. (See bottom photo, opposite page.)

On the drill press. Admittedly the most labor-intensive of all mortising operations, cutting mortises on the drill press is nevertheless a very satisfying way to construct this half of the mortise-and-tenon joint. Begin by laying out the mortise on your stock. Chuck a brad-point bit in the press equal to (or slightly less than) the desired width of the mortise, and set the depth stop to the depth of the mortise. (You can do this by marking the desired mortise depth on the side of the

Start at the ends. Cut the ends of the mortise first, plunging full-depth with each cut.

Move to the middle. Remove the waste by moving the table sideways and plunging in successive passes until you've cut the entire mortise.

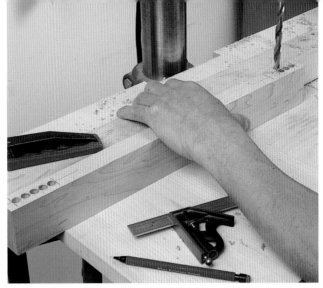

Drill side-by-side. Use a brad-point bit to remove most of the waste, drilling a series of holes without overlapping the cuts.

stock, then placing the stock next to the bit as you set the drill press stop.) Clamp a fence to the drill press table such that the stock is centered over the bit. Starting at one end of the mortise, drill straight down to the bottom of the mortise. Move the stock sideways, and drill another hole as close to the first hole as possible, but without overlapping it. (See photo, above.) Continue in this manner until you reach the opposite end of the mortise. Finish the joint at the bench by paring the sides of the mortise flat with a wide chisel, then squaring the ends using a chisel equal to the mortise's width.

Ready for a tenon. The finished mortise has rough but serviceable walls, with square ends to fit a traditional square-sided tenon.

Cutting Shoulders on the Table Saw

YOU CAN CUT tenon shoulders in several ways using a variety of machines, including the table saw, the router, and the bandsaw. However, if you're already using the table saw to make the cheek cuts, it's usually best to saw the shoulders on the same machine. The traditional approach is to lay the stock flat on the saw's table and crosscut the long shoulders using a miter gauge or the single-runner sled (see page 20). A standard saw blade works fine if you take a series of nibbling cuts, setting the blade height so the tips of the teeth just meet the tenon stock. Use a stop block clamped to the rip fence to register the workpiece, and hold the stock securely as you push it over the blade. (See middle left photo, below.) To cut the smaller, secondary shoulders, use the sled again, but this time orient the workpiece on its edge to make the cut. (See bottom left photo, below.)

Another approach is to use the tenoning jig (see page 23), which is particularly sensible if you've previously set up the jig to cut the cheeks. The trick is simply to move the rip fence (and the jig) sideways after making the cheek cuts, so that the last cut removes the waste and defines the shoulder in the same pass. This method is simple and allows you to keep the blade height setting as it is without a tedious second setup. Plus, it works equally well when sawing straight or angled shoulders. (See photo, below.)

Long shoulder cut. Adjust the blade height so it just grazes the tenon, and use a stop block clamped to the rip fence to locate the shoulder.

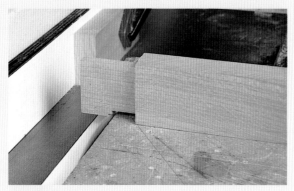

Smaller shoulders. Without changing the fence setting, crosscut the secondary shoulders with the workpiece on edge by taking a series of nibbling cuts.

Leave it in the jig. After sawing the cheeks, move the rip fence sideways to cut the shoulders. This technique works great for cutting 90° shoulders or for the angled shoulders shown here.

Where Tenons Meet

WHEN TWO rails meet at 90° into a post or leg, the tenons on the ends of the rails are likely to hit each other, or at least interfere with your ability to make long tenons. If the mortises in the post are located in relatively large stock, you might be fine. And in some framework, such as chair or table frames, adjoining rails can often be staggered from each other to solve the problem. But in many situations this isn't possible. When you're faced with two rails that intersect, the trick is to arrange the tenons before constructing the joint, so that they won't run into each other. Figure 5 shows three different approaches.

The first option is to offset the mortises toward the outside of the post, and then miter the ends of the tenons. This arrangement keeps the tenons long while avoiding interference. Another method is to cut a conventional long tenon on one piece, then cut two shorter tenons on the adjoining piece. The shorter tenons won't penetrate as deeply, but their extra glue surface will help compensate for this shortcoming. The last technique is to cut narrow tenons and let them pass over and under each other, adding haunches (short tenons) to prevent twisting. This reduces the tenons' overall width while maintaining their joint-strengthening length.

One note: It's important when laying out any of these intersecting mortise-and-tenon joints that you don't remove too much wood on the outside of the part that receives the mortise. Keeping mortise cheeks a minimum of ¼ inch thick in this area will prevent weakness in the joint.

FIG. 5 ▶ **Keeping the Joint Strong**

Mitered Tenons

Leave small gap between miters.

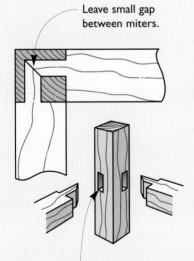

Offset mortises toward outside of stock to keep tenons long.

One Long; Two Short

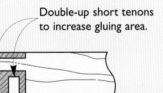

Double-up short tenons to increase gluing area.

Over and Under with Haunches

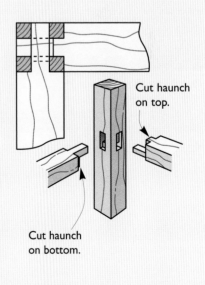

Cut haunch on top.

Cut haunch on bottom.

Bandsaw the haunch. Register the end of the tenon against the fence to cut the haunch's shoulder (top), then reset the fence to remove the waste (above).

Haunched Tenon

In Chinese furniture construction, there is a joint called "large-in, small-out." This is a version of the haunched joint, where a regular tenon is cut narrower across its width, and a smaller tenon or stub tenon is left to engage a smaller pocket that's part of a larger stepped mortise. This approach solves the problem of two rails (and their accompanying tenons) that meet at right angles to each other in the same post. This way, the rails can join the post at the same height while keeping the post strong.

Haunched tenons work not only in posts or other open framework to solve the problem of intersecting rails, but are a good choice for frame-and-panel construction. Here, the haunched area makes it easy to fit a panel to the frame because the resulting groove for the panel that goes

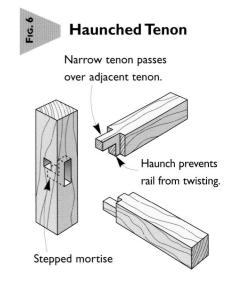

FIG. 6 **Haunched Tenon**

Narrow tenon passes over adjacent tenon.

Haunch prevents rail from twisting.

Stepped mortise

through the top of the post or stile is filled with the haunched area of the tenon. This makes construction much easier, while maintaining the integrity of the joint and providing resistance to racking. The drawing below shows a typical layout.

Frame-and-Panel Haunch

A HAUNCHED tenon is a good choice when making frame-and-panel assemblies to fill the gap at the ends of the stiles.

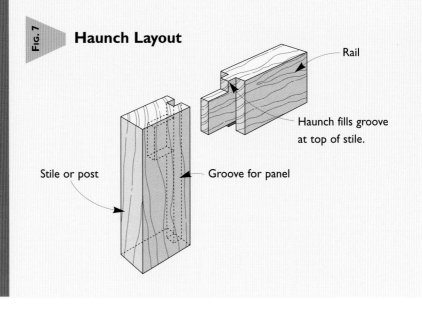

FIG. 7 **Haunch Layout**

Rail

Haunch fills groove at top of stile.

Stile or post

Groove for panel

Constructing a haunched tenon can be done on a variety of machines, but is best accomplished on the table saw or the bandsaw. The accompanying stepped mortise is cut with the hollow-chisel mortiser, a hand-held router, or on the drill press. (See Basic Mortise-and-Tenon, page 117.)

On the table saw. Begin by cutting a standard tenon, using one of the two approaches for milling a basic mortise-and-tenon (see page 117). Once you've cut the cheeks of the tenon, cut the two long shoulders with the tenoning jig or with a cutoff sled (see Cutting Shoulders on the Table Saw, page 112). Then cut the haunch with a standard saw blade or a dado blade, laying the stock on edge on the single-runner sled (see page 20) and removing enough material to leave at least half of the tenon width. Make the haunched area about ¼ inch long, or if you're cutting the joint for frame-and-panel construction, match the haunch length with the depth of the panel groove.

On the bandsaw. Cut the cheeks using a fence clamped to the table and following the same procedure as when cutting a slip joint (see page 113). Then cut the long shoulders by reading just the fence to the desired tenon length and positioning the stock on edge. The technique is the same as when cutting a basic mortise-and-tenon (see page 117).

Finish the tenon by laying out the haunch, then either cut to your layout lines by eye, or make the crosscut and rip cuts by resetting the fence for each cut, as shown in the photos on the opposite page. If you're building a frame and panel, be sure to cut the haunch so it matches the depth of the groove for the panel.

FIG. 7

Haunch-Mitered Tenon

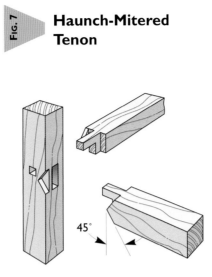

45°

Haunch-Mitered Tenon

The haunched-mitered tenon is part mortise-and-tenon and part lap joint. Typically found in many styles of Chinese furniture, the joint is especially useful in framework for cabinets and casework, where strength is needed and the appealing detail of a miter is desired for beauty. The haunched part of the joint allows two rails to meet in the same post without interference. Although it looks complicated, the joint is actually very straightforward if you approach the cutting sequence one step at a time. You can cut the tenons on the table saw or the bandsaw. See Basic Mortise-and-Tenon on page 117 for directions on cutting the stepped mortises.

On the table saw. Start by making the cheek cuts (for the tenon and the lap) and the shoulder cut (for the tenon), using the tenoning jig and same the approach as when making multiple tenons (see page 113). Cut the 45°

miters using a similar technique to the one used when making a mitered-corner lap (see page 96), laying the stock on the single-runner sled against a 45° fence. Adjust the blade height so it cuts through the lap, and not into the tenon. Make the first miter cut with the stock against one side of the fence; the second miter cut is made from the opposite side and should center the tip of the miter on the center of the stock. Then cut the haunch by laying the stock on edge on the single-runner sled (see page 20), leaving half the width of the tenon.

Once you've cut the stepped mortise, lay out the pocket for the mitered lap and cut it by hand with a chisel. Some final trimming and fitting is usually necessary to get a good fit.

On the bandsaw. Make the cheek cuts and the shoulder cut by guiding the work against a bandsaw fence, using the same method as when cutting a slip joint (see page 113). Lay out the haunch and cut it by eye, or use the fence and the same approach as when cutting a standard haunched tenon (see previous page). Now lay out the miter, and cut to your layout lines by eye.

After cutting the stepped mortise, lay out the pocket and cut it by hand with a chisel. Some final trimming is usually necessary to get a good fit.

Adjacent Tenons

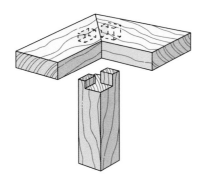

Loose Tenons

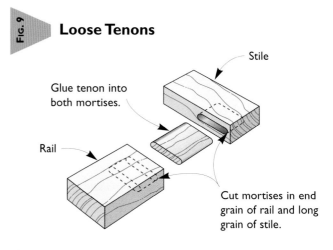

Stile

Glue tenon into both mortises.

Rail

Cut mortises in end grain of rail and long grain of stile.

Adjacent Tenons

Adjacent tenons are a good solution when you need to join two frame pieces to the end of a post, such as the frame of a tabletop. In traditional Chinese furniture, the tenons are formed on the same post or leg and connect two mitered frame pieces above. This arrangement has the advantage of locking the frame pieces to the post and keeps the miter joint from separating once the pieces are joined to the post. You can cut the tenons on the table or the bandsaw. In this particular case, it's best to cut the tenons first, fit the miters, then lay out and cut the mortises. Use the hollow-chisel mortiser, a hand-held router, or the drill press to cut the mortises. (See Basic Mortise-and-Tenon, page 117.)

On the table saw. Use the tenoning jig and the same technique used when making a slip joint (see page 113). The difference here is that you need to turn the stock 90° after sawing the first tenon cheek to cut the second, adjacent cheek. When cutting the second cheek, you will cut through the first tenon. This is fine, because the next step is to remove the waste by hand with a chisel, reducing each tenon to half its original width.

On the bandsaw. Use a bandsaw fence and the same approach as when cutting a slip joint (see page 113) to make the cheek cuts. After sawing the first cheek, turn the stock 90° and saw the second cheek, which will cut into the first cheek. Then remove the waste by hand with a chisel, reducing each tenon to half its original width.

Loose Tenon

The loose-tenon joint is a wonderful alternative to making a traditional mortise-and-tenon joint. Instead of cutting an integral tenon on the end of the rail, you cut a mortise. This mortise and a matching mortise in the stile or post accepts a separate "loose" tenon, which is glued into both mortises. The resulting joint is just as strong as a regular mortise-and-tenon. One of the advantages to using loose-tenon joinery is the ease with which you can connect parts at odd angles, since you don't have to mill angled shoulders on a tenon.

When making this joint, it's good to choose the same kind of wood for the loose tenon as you use on the frame pieces. Once you've milled the mortises, making the tenon stock is simple, as described in Making Loose Tenons, page 128. You can cut the mortises with a hand-held router, the mortising-and-tenoning fixture, or the hollow-chisel mortiser.

With a hand-held router. Clamp the rail stock in a bench vise with the end of the work flush with the benchtop. If you're working with angled stock, you can clamp the stock at the correct angle by making sure the end of the piece is level with the surface of the bench, as shown in the top photo, opposite page. Lay out the ends of the mortise on the end of the stock. Install a straight bit in a plunge router, and set the depth of cut to the desired depth of the mortise. Clamp a straightedge (a piece of plywood or MDF is fine) parallel to and at the correct distance from the workpiece so that the router bit is centered on the stock.

Now ride the base of the router against the edge of the straightedge, making a series of ⅛-inch-deep plunge cuts into the work and moving the router forward until you reach

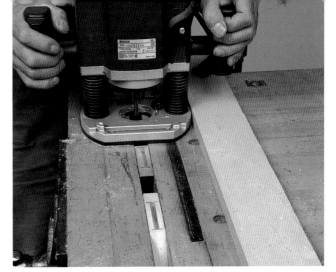

Plunging end grain. Set the router's depth stop and plunge-cut the mortise by guiding the router against a straightedge.

the layout marks at the end of the mortise. Keep cutting in this manner until you reach the full depth of the mortise. Use the same approach to cut the long-grain mortise in the stile or post, which is the same routing technique as when cutting a basic mortise-and-tenon (see page 117).

With the mortising-and-tenoning fixture. Lay out the ends of the mortise on the face of your stock, then clamp the stock perpendicular to the fixture's fence. Adjust the length of the bit to correspond to the desired mortise depth, and set the height so the bit is centered on the stock. Push the stock into the spinning bit in ⅛-inch increments while moving it sideways, stopping at your layout marks, as shown in the middle photo, right. Continue routing in this manner until the stock contacts the fence.

With the hollow-chisel mortiser. Lay out the ends of the mortise on the end of the stock, and clamp the stock vertically in the machine's vise. (You'll have to reorient the machine's fence parallel with the bit in order to do this.) Start at each end of the mortise, plunging straight down and then pulling up to cut a square pocket, as shown in the photo, right. Remove the waste in the middle by moving the table and plunging in successive passes, taking overlapping cuts until you've cut the entire mortise. Note that with this approach you'll end up with square mortises, so you don't have to round over the tenon stock, which keeps things simple.

End-grain slot. Cut in ⅛-inch-deep increments, moving the stock sideways until the bit reaches your layout marks.

Chiseling the end. Reposition the fence vertically, then cut the ends first and finish in the middle.

Making Loose Tenons

THE LOOSE-TENON joint consists of two mortises connected by a separate loose tenon. (See Loose Tenon, page 126.) For the joint to be successful, the tenon must fit tightly in the mortises. The procedure for making the tenon is simple.

I always start with extra-long stock, which allows me to make multiple tenons from the same stock. Begin by preparing the stock to width so it corresponds to the exact length of your mortises, and rip or thickness-plane the stock until it slides snugly into one of the mortises. If you've cut the mortises with a router bit, its ends will be rounded, and you'll need to shape the tenon stock to fit. Do this by selecting a roundover bit with a radius equal to the curvature in your mortises. For example, if you used a 1/2-inch bit to rout the mortises, choose a 1/4-inch roundover bit. Chuck the bit in the router table and rout all four edges of your tenon stock.

The last step is to cut individual tenons to length. First measure the depth of each mortise and combine the two measurements. Subtract 1/16 inch from the combined measurement, and cut your tenon stock to this length on the table saw using a cutoff sled and a stop. The extra 1/16 inch gives you some breathing room for excess glue and ensures the shoulders of the joints come together cleanly.

FIG. 10

Cutting the Stock

1. Cut mortises in stock, then rip or plane overlong blank to fit mortise width and length.

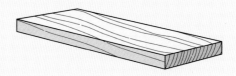

2. Round over long edges on router table.

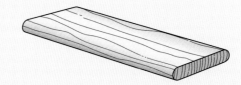

3. Crosscut tenons to length.

Cut individual tenons to combined depth of two mortises minus 1/16 in.

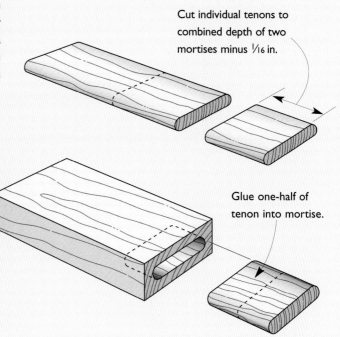

Glue one-half of tenon into mortise.

Rounding Over the Tenon Blank

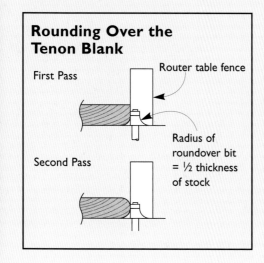

First Pass

Router table fence

Second Pass

Radius of roundover bit = 1/2 thickness of stock

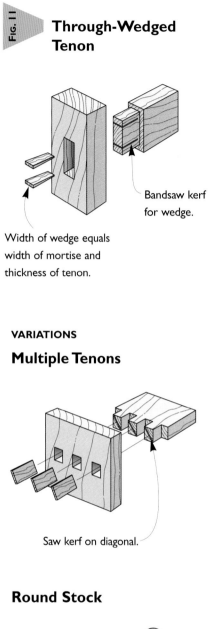

FIG. 11 Through-Wedged Tenon

Bandsaw kerf for wedge.

Width of wedge equals width of mortise and thickness of tenon.

VARIATIONS

Multiple Tenons

Saw kerf on diagonal.

Round Stock

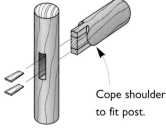

Cope shoulder to fit post.

Through-Wedged Tenon

A through-wedged tenon has a distinctly visual appeal and makes a very dramatic statement. It is also one of the strongest types of mortise-and-tenon joints, because the wedges ensure a tight-fitting connection even if the glue should someday fail. You can use this joint for practically every type of woodworking, from framework to casework. The standard through-wedged tenon works best for frames, such as where a rail meets a post in a table. Cutting multiple tenons is a great way to join case parts, such as where a partition meets the middle of a case side. Even round stock, such as the rounded frame of a chair or table, can benefit from a wedged tenon, although the construction is a little trickier since you need to cope the rail to fit seamlessly into the rounded face of the post.

A variety of machines can be used to construct this joint, from the table saw, bandsaw, and router to the hollow-chisel mortiser and drill press. You can use one or multiple wedges in each joint, making them from the same wood as the project or using a contrasting wood for a stronger visual effect. Saw slots, or kerfs, into the end of the tenon to fit the wedges. One note: Be sure to orient the slots in the tenon so the wedging action bears against the end-grain of the post to avoid splitting. Dimension the wedges so their width fits the mortise opening, and make them slightly less than the length of your tenons. You can taper the wedge from almost nothing to ⅛ or ¼ inch thick, using an angle of about 10°. Thicker wedges are harder to fit, and risk splitting the tenon. Cut the wedges on the bandsaw, or use the table saw and a cutoff sled equipped with an angled fence.

A word about making the joint in round stock: The construction sequence is easiest if you cut both the tenon and the mortise while the stock is still square. Once you've cut the joints, round over the stock with a hand plane and spokeshave, or on the router table with the appropriate sized roundover bit.

On the table saw. There are two approaches for cutting the tenons on the table saw, depending on the type of through-tenon joint you're making. For a single, standard tenon, use the same approach as when cutting a basic mortise-and-tenon (see page 117), and make sure to cut shoulders on all four sides. For multiple tenons, use the same approach as when cutting standard finger joints (see page 87), standing the work vertically on the double-runner sled and making the cuts with a dado blade. Use the finger-joint jig (see page 87) if you want evenly spaced tenons. To vary the spacing, simply lay out the tenons on the stock and use a tall fence screwed to the sled to support the stock, then line up the blade to your marks.

Look to the router, hollow-chisel mortiser, or drill press to cut the mating mortises. Make the wedges, then saw kerfs in the ends of the tenons for the wedges. Depending on the thickness of your wedges at their narrow ends, you can use either the table saw, the bandsaw, or a handsaw to cut the slots.

On the bandsaw. Use a fence and the same method as when cutting a slip joint (see page 113) to cut the tenons. If you're making multiple tenons, lay them out and cut them either freehand or by resetting the fence for each cut.

Classic Joints with Power Tools **129**

Carving shoulders. Start at the shoulder, swinging the stock around the blade to cut the overall curve (top). Then refine the inside corners by holding the stock square to the blade and moving the work sideways, taking light, skimming cuts (above).

For a rounded through-tenon, first lay out the joint on your square rail stock, outlining the tenon location and using a compass set to the radius of the post stock to mark the curved shoulders on the rail. Cut the tenon using the same method as when cutting a slip joint (see page 113). Then bandsaw the curved shoulders free-hand, following your layout lines. (See photos, left.)

Once you've cut the mortise in the post and rounded both the post and the rail, cut the wedges form the wood of your choice. To cut the kerfs for the wedges, simply hold a piece of straight-edged plywood in one hand roughly parallel to the blade while feeding the work into the blade with the other hand, stopping the cut about ⅛ inch from the tenon shoulder. (See bottom left photo, below.) It's wise to always check the fit of the wedges in the tenon before gluing and assembling the joint. They should tap in easily with soft blows from a hammer. (See photo, below.)

With a hand-held router. Cutting through-mortises for multiple through-tenons with a plunge router is a great technique that simplifies making this half of the joint. Lay out the mortises on the stock, then lay a piece of scrap under the stock and clamp the assembly to your workbench. Equip your router with a straight bit whose diameter equals the finished width of the mortise. Clamp the dado jig (see page 26) to one edge of your mortise layout, and set up a stop block to limit the length of each mortise. Cut the mortises by following the jig with the base of the router, taking a series of ⅛-inch-deep cuts until you rout through the work and slightly into the scrap beneath. (See photo, below.) Finish by either squaring the ends of the mortises with a chisel or rounding the edges of the tenons with a file.

With the hollow-chisel mortiser. While most mortisers won't allow you to cut case mortises in wide panels, this is an excellent machine for milling through-mortises in narrow frame

Kerf for wedges. Guide the cut by holding a straight piece of plywood in line with the blade and sliding the work against the plywood. Stop about ⅛ inch from the shoulder.

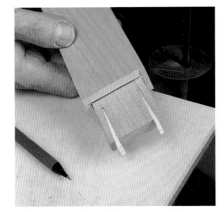

Check the fit. Before assembling the joint, tap in the wedges to make sure they fit.

Routing to the other side. Guide the router against the dado jig, regulating mortise length with a stop block. Place scrap under the work or hang the work over the benchtop to avoid routing into your bench.

members, such as for a through-tenon joint in round stock. Use the same milling technique used for cutting a basic mortise-and-tenon (see page 117), but make sure to back up the bottom of the workpiece with scrap so the bit will exit the workpiece cleanly and without damage.

On the drill press. The drill press is a good choice if you need to make multiple mortises in case parts. Use the same setup as when drilling an end-to-face dowel joint (see page 73), using a fence and drilling all the holes in half of the panel, then reorienting the stock 180° on the table and drilling the remaining holes. First lay out the mortises, then choose a bit whose diameter is equal to, or slightly less than, the desired width of the mortise. Set the depth stop on the press so the bit just exits the back side of the workpiece. Then drill a series of holes through each mortise, using the same technique as when making a basic mortise-and-tenon (see page 117). Finish the mortises by paring their sides flat and their ends square.

Pegging A Mortise-and-Tenon Joint

▶ **A PEGGED** mortise-and-tenon joint can hold parts together if the glue should ever fail. Plus, pegs offer opportunities for decorative effects. You can turn your own pegs on the lathe from any wood you like, use a brass rod, buy bamboo skewers, or whittle square heads on round pegs.

You can use a single peg, or two or more pegs per joint. Generally, it's best to use pegs between $\frac{1}{8}$ and $\frac{1}{4}$ inch in diameter. For small work, $\frac{1}{8}$-inch bamboo skewers make excellent pegs, since bamboo is very stiff and can bend and flex without breaking. Locate your pegs close to the shoulder, or about $\frac{3}{8}$ inch from the edge of the stile or post. Paired or multiple pegs should be spaced as wide apart as possible.

Add the pegs after assembling the joint. Mark and drill through the joint with the appropriate sized brad-point bit. Be sure to back up the work with a scrap block to avoid tearing out the back of the joint. Make your pegs slightly longer than the thickness of the work. To install a peg, place a dab of glue around the end of the peg (use epoxy if your pegs are brass or another metal), and tap it into the hole so it extends slightly past the opposite face. Once the glue has dried, use a handsaw or a sharp chisel (or a hacksaw for metal) to trim the peg flush with the joint.

Fig. 12

▶ **Peg Options**

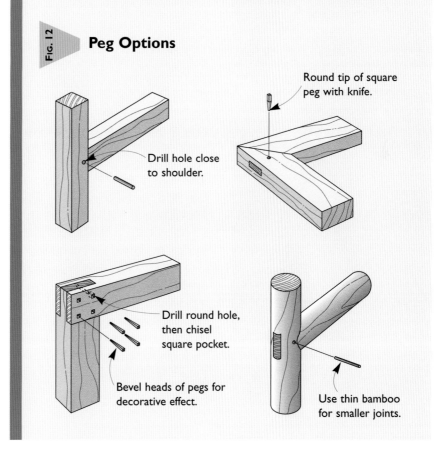

Drill hole close to shoulder.

Round tip of square peg with knife.

Drill round hole, then chisel square pocket.

Bevel heads of pegs for decorative effect.

Use thin bamboo for smaller joints.

FIG. 13

Angled Tenon

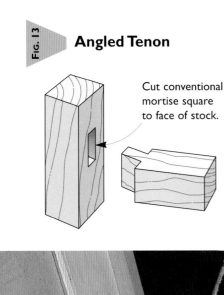

Cut conventional mortise square to face of stock.

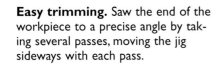

Easy trimming. Saw the end of the workpiece to a precise angle by taking several passes, moving the jig sideways with each pass.

Cheeks and shoulders. Raise the blade to the desired tenon length and saw the cheeks and the shoulders in a succession of cuts, moving the jig sideways after each pass.

Angled Tenon

In many situations, a rail joint is not at a right angle. The best example is in chairs, especially where a trapezoidal seat frame meets the legs. Cutting an angled mortise would solve the problem, but is a lot of trouble. The answer is to angle the tenon instead, which allows you to cut a standard mortise. (See Basic Mortise-and-Tenon, page 117.) When making an angled tenon, be aware that there is a limit to the angle you can produce. The more the angle, the more you will create short grain in the tenon, which significantly weakens the tenon itself. Therefore try to keep the angles of your tenons to a minimum for strength. The joint is most easily cut on the table saw.

On the table saw. Use the adjustable angled fence (see page 22) to position the rail stock at the desired angle to the blade. To prevent cutting into the jig using this technique, clamp or screw a scrap panel to the jig's fence. Once you've set up the fence, clamp the stock perpendicular to the saw table and against the scrap panel. Now use the jig itself to trim the ends of your stock to the angle of the jig by taking a series of ⅛- to ¼-inch-deep cuts with a standard blade, moving the jig after each pass until you've trimmed the entire end. (See top left photo, above.)

Reclamp the stack with its sawn end on the table. Cut the tenon by sawing one cheek, then move the jig sideways and make a series of cuts to remove the waste and create one shoulder. Then saw the second cheek parallel to the first and remove the waste up to the shoulder by moving the jig as before, as shown in the photo, left.

FIG. 14

Mitered Corner with Through-Tenon

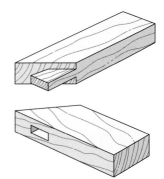

Mitered Corner with Through-Tenon

The mitered corner with through-tenon is used widely in Chinese furniture, especially in frame-and-panel construction. This joint is aesthetically pleasing, since you get the strength of a mortise-and-tenon joint without showing all of the end grain on one side, thanks the miter cut. In addition, wood movement is kept to a minimum because the two parts of the joint will swell and shrink in unison without placing stress on the joint. The table saw and the bandsaw work in combination to make this joint.

On the table saw. The first step is to cut the mortise, which can be done with a hand-held router, the hollow-chisel mortiser, or the drill press. (See Basic Mortise-and-Tenon, page 117.) Generally, I make the mortise length equal to one-half the width of the stock I'm working with. It's easiest if you keep the stock overlong for now, and locate the mortise further in from the end of the stock. Once you've cut the mortise, use the single-runner sled equipped with a 45° fence (see page 20) to miter the end of the mortise

Mortise, then miter. Cut the miter after mortising the workpiece, lining up the blade with the inner end of the mortise.

FIG. 15

Double Miter

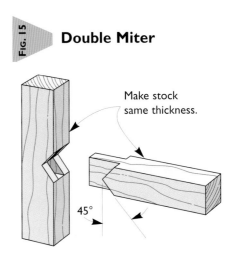

Make stock same thickness.

45°

piece, trimming the end precisely at the inner end of the mortise, as shown in the photo, above.

Miter the tenon piece and form its tenon using the same setup as when cutting a mitered slip joint (see page 116), holding the stock at 45° to the blade and using the tenoning jig. Trim the tenon to fit the mortise on the bandsaw.

On the bandsaw. Once the tenon is formed and the miter cut, you can cut the tenon freehand on the bandsaw to fit the mortise. First rip the tenon to a width that corresponds to the length of the mortise, then remove the waste by following close to—but slightly away from—the mitered shoulder line. (See photo, below.) Finish by chiseling the shoulder smooth.

Double Miter

The double miter is a good choice when joining a rail in the center of another piece, such as where a horizontal rail meets a vertical post. The tenon is made on the table saw; the mortise can be cut with a hand-held router, the hollow-chisel mortiser, or on the drill press (see Basic Mortise-and-Tenon, page 117), then you'll cut its miter on the table saw.

On the table saw. Use the tenoning jig equipped with an angled fence and the same approach as when cutting a mitered slip joint (see page 116), to cut the tenon and the 45° mitered shoulders. Make two cuts on each face, reorienting the workpiece after the first cut to the opposite side of the fence to cut the opposing miter. Move the jig sideways as necessary until you've formed the cheeks of the tenon and the mitered shoulders.

Once you've cut the mortise in the adjoining piece, use the single-runner sled (see page 20) to cut the miter or "bird's mouth" notch. Hold the stock on edge against the 90° fence, tilt the saw blade to 45°, and raise the blade so it's tip lands in the center of the stock. Turn the stock around and make the second miter cut to free the waste.

Bandsaw by hand. Trim the tenon on the bandsaw, working freehand by following the mitered shoulder line.

Fig. 16

Three-Way Miter

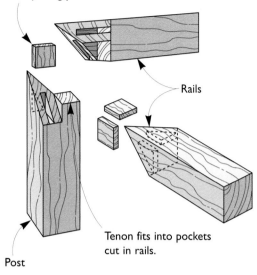

Loose tenon fits slot
cut in adjoining pieces.

Rails

Tenon fits into pockets
cut in rails.

Post

Three-Way Miter

Joining three rails together in the traditional manner results in one member showing end grain, no matter how you arrange the parts. To solve this aesthetic dilemma, Chinese craftsman hundreds of years ago created the traditional three-way miter joint. It is a sound, mechanical joint with all of its end grain concealed. Because of its clever design, wood movement will occur at an equal rate and in the same direction, helping keep the joint strong for a long time. The joint described here is not constructed in the traditional manner, but has been modified slightly to make it simple to cut with power tools.

The main concern when constructing this joint is to ensure your stock is prepared to the same width and thickness, and to make sure all sides are perfectly square. Any amount of out-of-square will result in miters exhibiting small openings or cracks when the joint is assembled. The good thing is that the entire joint can be constructed on the table saw, with the exception of cutting the slots for the loose tenons. You can cut these small mortises by hand with a chisel or with the hollow-chisel mortiser (see Basic Mortise-and-Tenon, page 117).

Order of Construction

FOLLOW the sequence of steps below to construct a three-way miter.

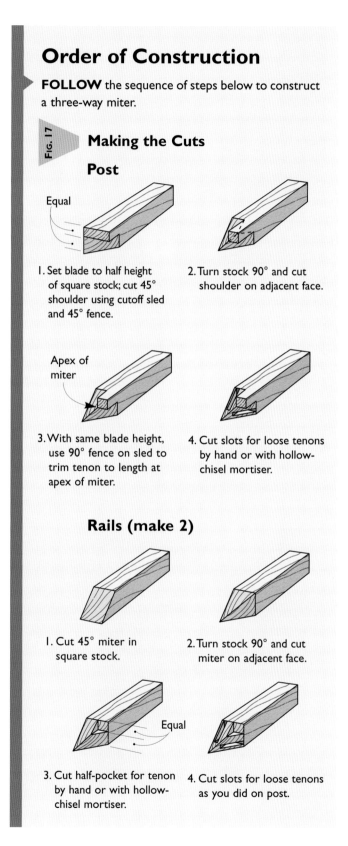

Fig. 17

Making the Cuts

Post

Equal

1. Set blade to half height of square stock; cut 45° shoulder using cutoff sled and 45° fence.

2. Turn stock 90° and cut shoulder on adjacent face.

Apex of miter

3. With same blade height, use 90° fence on sled to trim tenon to length at apex of miter.

4. Cut slots for loose tenons by hand or with hollow-chisel mortiser.

Rails (make 2)

1. Cut 45° miter in square stock.

2. Turn stock 90° and cut miter on adjacent face.

Equal

3. Cut half-pocket for tenon by hand or with hollow-chisel mortiser.

4. Cut slots for loose tenons as you did on post.

On the table saw. Figure 17 shows the sequence of cuts you'll make. You can start with the post or with the two rails; the particular order isn't important. On the post, first raise the blade to half the stock height, and cut a 45° shoulder using the single-runner sled equipped with a 45° fence (see page 20). Then turn the post 90° and use the sled again to cut the adjacent shoulder, freeing the waste piece.

Without changing the blade height, place the post on the jig's 90° fence and trim the tenon to length. Cut the slots by hand or with a hollow chisel.

On each rail, raise the blade above the stock and first cut a 45° miter on one face using the single-runner sled and the 45° fence. (For more on cutting miters, see Jigs for Accurate Joints, page 20.) Then turn the rail 90° and cut a miter on the adjacent face. Finish up by cutting the pocket for the tenon and the slots for the loose tenons as mentioned above.

Knock-Down Mortise-and-Tenon

While the majority of mortise-and-tenon joints require glue for a strong bond, there is a class of joints that work equally well without any glue at all. In fact, adding glue to most of these joints defeats their main purpose, which is the ability to take the joint apart after assembly. These knock-down joints offer plenty of strength, yet the option of disassembly is very handy in many furnituremaking situations—taking a large bed frame apart for transport, or delivering and installing a run of large cabinets that would normally be impractical to build as a unit.

You can choose from three types of knock-down mortise-and-tenon joints: a doweled tenon, where the wedge-shaped half-dowel locks the tenon to the mortise; a wedged tenon, where the wedge works in similar fashion to keep the joint tight; and a stub tenon with a nut and bolt that works via either a metal nut and washer or a cylinder nut.

FIG. 18

Knock-Down Mortise and Tenon

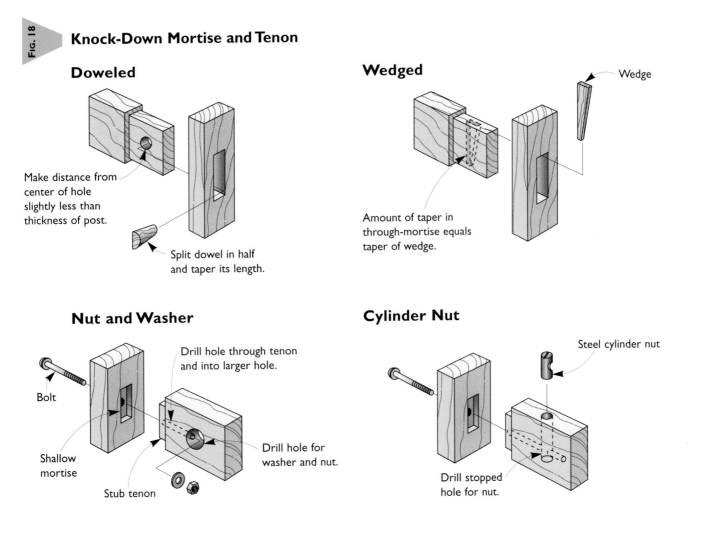

Doweled

Make distance from center of hole slightly less than thickness of post.

Split dowel in half and taper its length.

Wedged

Wedge

Amount of taper in through-mortise equals taper of wedge.

Nut and Washer

Drill hole through tenon and into larger hole.

Bolt

Shallow mortise

Stub tenon

Drill hole for washer and nut.

Cylinder Nut

Steel cylinder nut

Drill stopped hole for nut.

Of the three varieties, the metal connectors offer superior strength, and are a good choice for joining really heavy frames (such as the bed frame mentioned above) or where repeated assembly and disassembly is expected. The wooden dowel or wedge versions offer good strength while allowing you to create a decorative effect in your project, making them more suited to fine furniture.

All three joints are simple to construct, and can be made using conventional machine methods on the table saw, bandsaw, router, mortising-and-tenoning fixture, hollow-chisel mortiser, or the drill press. Make the wedge-shaped half-dowel by splitting a dowel in half and tapering it 10° on a belt sander or with a hand plane and chisel. Make the wooden wedge such that it's one-third the thickness of the tenon, and taper it to 10° as well on the bandsaw.

On the table saw. Use the tenoning jig and the same approach as when cutting a basic mortise-and-tenon (see page 117) to cut the tenons on any one of the three joints. The dowel and the wedge joint require extra-long tenons, so make sure you design the joint to accommodate the limitations of your table saw's blade height, which is usually about 3 inches. You should leave at least 1½ inches of material on the tenon where it extends beyond the mortise.

If your design calls for a really long tenon, an alternative method is to make it using a dado blade and the double-runner sled, as described for cutting a basic mortise-and-tenon.

If you're making a knock-down joint with a stub tenon, the tenon (and the mortise) doesn't need to be very deep, as its main purpose is to register the parts and keep them from racking. A tenon length of ½ inch is usually sufficient.

On the bandsaw. Use a fence and the same technique used when making the basic mortise-and-tenon (see page 117) to cut the tenons on the bandsaw.

With a hand-held router. Cut the through-mortise using the identical setup as when making a through-wedged tenon (see page 129), plunging through the stock with a straight bit and guiding the router against the dado jig. Cut the shallow mortise (for the stub-tenon joint) using the same approach as when cutting a basic mortise-and-tenon (see page 117).

You have the option of either squaring the ends of the mortise with a chisel to fit the tenon, or rounding the edges of the tenon with a file to fit the rounded ends of the mortise.

With the mortising-and-tenoning fixture. You can cut the through-mortise, shallow mortise, and long or short tenons with this device. Setup and use is identical to cutting a basic mortise-and-tenon (see page 117). To avoid routing into the fixture's fence when cutting the through-mortise, screw or temporarily glue a piece of thin plywood to the face of the fence and rout into that instead.

With the hollow-chisel mortiser. Cut the through-mortise or the shallow mortise using the same method as for a basic mortise-and-tenon (see page 117). You can also use the mortiser to cut the through-mortise in the tenon that accepts the wedge. Locate the mortise first by assembling the joint and marking where the tenon extends beyond the face of the post, then cut the mortise to its shorter length. Finish by lengthening the mortise at one end and tapering it to 10° with sloping cuts from a chisel.

On the drill press. Use the drill press to drill the hole in the tenon for the dowel joint, sizing the hole so it's roughly the same diameter as the center section of the wedge-shaped dowel. This ensures the dowel will enter the hole easily during assembly, yet lock the joint tight when tapped fully into position. Locate the dowel hole by assembling the joint, and marking where the tenon extends beyond the face of the post. Position the centerline of the hole about 1/16 inch back from this line, and drill your hole to that mark.

You're best off boring the long hole for the bolt in the stub-tenon joint with a hand drill. Do this by assembling the joint, then drilling through the post and into the rail. However, you can use the drill press for drilling the hole for the nut and washer, sizing the hole so it accommodates the diameter of the washer. If you're using a cylinder nut, bore this hole into the rail on the drill press, too. Be sure to set your depth stop to drill a stopped hole such that when the nut is installed, the threaded hole inside the cylinder lines up with the bolt hole. This arrangement will make assembly much easier.

Fox-Wedged Tenon

Wedges are great for locking a mortise-and-tenon joint, such as the through-wedged tenon shown on page 129. But in situations where your design won't allow for a through-joint, where the tenon is exposed, you can still use wedges by making a fox-wedged joint. With this type of joint, the wedges (and the end of the tenon) are never seen. You should be aware that there is some risk when constructing this joint. Everything must be cut and fitted correctly, or the joint may not close properly—and you won't get the opportunity to fix your mistake, since assembly is a one-shot affair! But the joint is interesting and has its advantages, especially for situations where you need a lot of strength, such as when attaching door or drawer pulls with round tenons. Construction is straightforward, and both the tenon and the mortise can be cut using the same methods and machines used for making a basic mortise-and-tenon (see page 117).

Once you've milled the mortise and the tenon, make the wedges and cut kerfs into the end of the tenon on the bandsaw, table saw, or with a handsaw. Then use a chisel to slightly undercut the end walls of the mortise. This will allow the tenon to flare slightly when the wedges do their work, locking the joint tight.

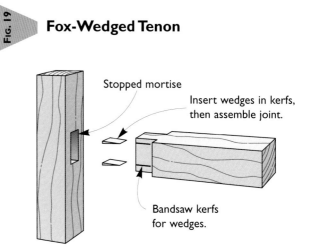

FIG. 19

Fox-Wedged Tenon

Stopped mortise

Insert wedges in kerfs, then assemble joint.

Bandsaw kerfs for wedges.

FIG. 1

DOVETAIL JOINTS

Through-Dovetails

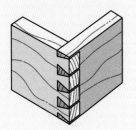

Mock Dovetails

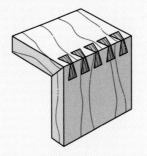

Dovetail Keys

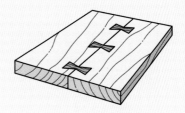

Mitered Through-Dovetails

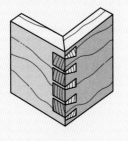

Sliding Dovetail

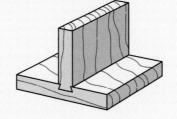

Half-Blind Dovetails

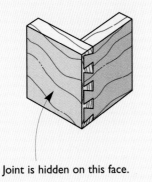

Joint is hidden on this face.

VARIATION

Tapered Sliding Dovetail

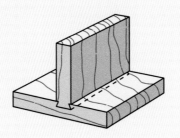

Dovetail Joints

The dovetail is a traditional joint that's been used for many centuries. It's also one of the most attractive joints in woodworking. Consisting of tails and pins (or sockets, depending on the specific type of dovetail), the joint gets its name from the distinctive shape of its parts, which resemble the flared tail of a dove. In addition to being beautiful and showing fine craftsmanship, the joint's mechanical wedging effect makes it very strong. In fact, you can assemble the parts without any means of reinforcement, including glue if you need to. Traditionally, dovetail joints are used for all sorts of box-type constructions, including corner joints for casework and drawers, and for joining wide panels in the middle of other panels, such as dividers and partitions. One specialty joint—dovetail keys—can be used when joining panels edge-to-edge, adding a decorative element while providing a mechanical link.

Depending on the type of dovetail joint you choose, you have the option of concealing the dovetails or showing off your handiwork. Another consideration is the specific dovetail angle you use, which can affect the strength of the joint as well as its appearance (see Useful Dovetail Angles, right).

One question novice woodworkers often ask is whether to cut the pins or the tails first, and experts debate hotly over this issue when it comes to hand-cut dovetails. But because of the process involved when cutting this joint by machine, it's usually best to cut the tails first, then use the completed tails to help lay out the pins. For more on this approach, see Laying Out and Scribing Dovetails on page 142.

Many woodworkers already know that dovetails can be cut with a router and a dovetail bit, using either a commercial dovetail jig or with special setups and techniques on the router table and a hand-held router. But it may surprise you to learn that the table saw and the bandsaw are also excellent machines when it comes to making this time-honored joint.

Useful Dovetail Angles

CHOOSING the correct dovetail angle is an important consideration. While there isn't one perfect angle that all woodworkers use, there are a few guidelines that will help you decide which angle is best for you, based on two important factors: strength and beauty. A carefully chosen angle keeps the sharp tips of the tails strong; too severe of an angle results in weak short grain in this area. On the other hand, a shallow angle provides very little wedging effect and can compromise the mechanical strength of the joint. In addition, really shallow angles result in bland-looking dovetails without the unique visual appeal characteristic of this joint. The answer is to find a comfortable compromise.

If you're routing the joint with a commercial dovetail jig, your choice will be based on the specific dovetail bit, generally available in two angles: 7° or 14°. Either angle is fine, although you may want to consider the thickness of your stock when choosing one over the other and the type of work you're making, as shown in figure 2. If you prefer to cut the joint with another machine or setup, you have an infinite choice of angles, but it's generally best to keep the angle somewhere between these two extremes—7° and 14°—to keep your joints strong and good looking. When machining the joint on the table saw, bandsaw, router table, or hand-held router, I usually prefer an angle of about 12°. To my eye, the angle looks good and provides a strong mechanical connection, plus I find this angle helps with specific machine setups and keeps the construction process simple.

FIG. 2

Useful Dovetail Angles

Good angles are generally between 7° – 14°.

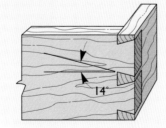 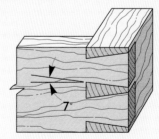

Use steeper angle when joining relatively thin parts.

Use shallower angle when joining thick parts.

FIG. 3

Through-Dovetails

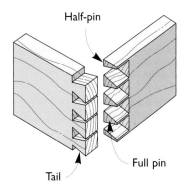

Half-pin

Full pin

Tail

Cut a straight line. Use a sharp knife and a square to mark the baseline.

Through-Dovetails

This is the most basic of all dovetail joints, and is typically used for connecting the corners of a drawer box as well as for bigger boxes in high-end cabinet construction. The joint is strong and steady, and will hold together with little or no glue. Since the tails and pins show on both sides of the joint, you can choose to display the joint as a design feature in the finished piece. Traditionally, moldings and other coverings were used to conceal the joinery. Power tools for through-dovetails include the table saw, bandsaw, router table, commercial dovetail jig, and hand-held router.

On the table saw. Begin by cutting the tails. Lay out the joint on your tail stock (see Laying Out and Scribing Dovetails, page 142). Although it's not essential, I like to scribe the baseline on all of my boards with a sharp knife before machining, as shown in the top photo, right. The incised line helps with setting the blade height accurately, reduces tearout during sawing, and provides a shoulder for subsequent chisel cuts.

Tilt the saw blade to the desired dovetail angle, then mount the double-runner sled (see page 21) on the saw and adjust the blade height to the baseline you scribed earlier. (Make sure the uppermost tips of the angled teeth meet the baseline, not above it.) Clamp the tail board vertically against the sled's fence, and, starting at one edge of the stock, line up the blade with the first dovetail cheek. Now push the assembly past the blade, making sure to cut to the waste side of your layout line. Continue in this fashion, cutting to one side of all your layout marks until you reach the opposite

One side of the tails. Tilt the blade to the dovetail angle and use the sled to saw one side of all the cheeks.

Second side. With the stock turned 180°, saw the opposite cheeks.

edge of the board. (See middle photo, opposite page.) Without changing the blade setup, turn the board 180° and repeat the cutting sequence on the opposite cheeks, as shown in the bottom photo, opposite page.

With all the cheeks cut, crank the blade 90° and make a series of cuts to remove as much of the waste between the cheeks as you can, again being careful not to cut into the baseline. (See photo, right.) Finish the tail board by cleaning out the remaining waste by hand with a chisel. Then use the completed tail board to transfer the pin locations onto the pin board.

Cut the pins next. With the saw blade still square to the table, remove the double-runner sled and screw a tall plywood or MDF fence to your miter gauge. Adjust the gauge to the same angle you used when tilting the saw blade. Make a few test cuts in scrap to check that the angle matches the cheek cuts you made earlier. Then clamp the pin board vertically to the fence on the miter gauge, and lower the blade height to the board's baseline. Follow the same cutting process as you did on the tail board, starting at one edge of the stock and making all the cheek cuts to one side of your layout lines. After cutting an individual cheek, make a few cuts beyond the cheek to remove the waste, but be careful not to cut too close to the adjacent cheek. (See photo, right.)

Complete the tails by turning the stock 180° and readjusting the miter gauge to a complementary dovetail angle. Follow the same cutting sequence as before, clamping the stock to the miter gauge and cutting the opposite cheeks, as shown in the bottom photo, right.

Cut the waste. Keep the blade at 90° to remove as much of the waste as possible.

And now the tails. Square the blade and use a high fence secured to the miter gauge to saw the pins, setting the gauge to the same angle as the tails.

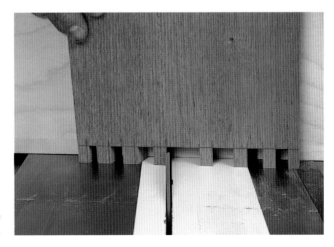

From the other side. Turn over the work and angle the gauge in the opposite direction to saw the opposite cheeks.

Laying Out and Scribing Dovetails

GOOD LAYOUT is the key to most machine-cut dovetail joints. Because of the machining sequence, it makes sense to cut the tails first, then use the tails to lay out the pins on the adjoining board. Start by using a square and a sharp knife, or a marking gauge, to scribe the baseline on your stock (you can calculate the baseline by measuring the thickness of the stock you're joining). Then set a bevel gauge to the desired dovetail angle, and mark the tails on one face with the gauge and a pencil. If necessary, use a small square to transfer the angles to the opposite face by squaring your lines across the end of the board and drawing the tails on the second face with the same gauge setting.

Consider the spacing of the joint when laying out the tails. You have the opportunity here for artistic expression. Start by leaving a half-pin on the edges. Tails can be spaced equally across the board's width, or you can vary the spacing, laying out wider tails near the center of the board and smaller tails near the edges. Either way, it's a good idea to keep the tails wider than the pins for good looks. And keep in mind that the narrowest area—usually the pin—must be wide enough to accommodate the width of the cutter you plan to use, be it saw blade or router bit. One tip: You'll avoid mistakes by marking each waste area with a few pencil strokes or an X to remind you of which area to cut.

Once you've cut the tails, use them to lay out the location of the pins. I find the easiest method is to clamp the pin board vertically in a bench vise, then position the tail board over the pin board, and trace around the tails with a mechanical pencil or a sharp, pointed knife. (See photo, below.) After transferring the angles, use a small square and a pencil to square your lines onto the face of the pin board for subsequent machining.

Tails First; Then Pins

Lay Out the Tails First

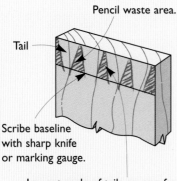

Pencil waste area.

Tail

Scribe baseline with sharp knife or marking gauge.

Lay out angle of tails on one face with bevel gauge. Space tails equally, or vary spacing if desired.

Scribe the Pins from the Tails

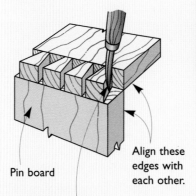

Pin board

Align these edges with each other.

Use cut tails to scribe end of pin board by tracing tails with pointed knife or slim pencil.

Good layout. Clamp the pin board in a vise and lay the tails over the stock to trace the angles, making sure the edges of both boards are aligned and the ends of the tails are flush.

Angle the work. An angled board cut to the dovetail angle moves with the workpiece when sawing the first cheek. Clamp another board to the saw table to stop the cut when the blade reaches the baseline.

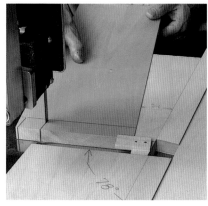

Spaced out. Without moving the fence, place a spacer between the angled board and the fence to cut the second cheek.

On the bandsaw. This technique works with the special pin-cutting jig shown in figure 5, next page. Because you use the thin blade of the bandsaw, you can cut very thin pins if you wish—a visual detail that adds great appeal to the joint. You'll start by cutting the tails first. First, scribe the baseline on your stock; it's not necessary to lay out the tails.

Lightly clamp a low fence (a piece of $3/4$ inch plywood works great) to the saw table, parallel to the blade, and place an angled board against the fence. The board should be slightly thinner than the thickness of the work, and sloped to the desired dovetail angle, with a small stop nailed at its narrow end. Now place the tail board against the angled board, and adjust the fence so that the far end of the workpiece is aligned with the blade to cut a half-pin. Tightly clamp the fence to the saw table. Finally, clamp a third board to the outfeed side of the table to act as a stop, with its end cut to a complementary angle. For example, in the photo shown above, top left, the angled board is cut to 12°, therefore the end of the stop is cut to 78°. Make sure the stop board is positioned such that it stops the workpiece when the saw blade reaches the baseline. Now cut the first cheek by pushing the workpiece and the angled board into the blade as one unit until the angled board contacts the stop.

For the next cheek cut, position a spacer between the angled board and the fence, making the spacer equal to the desired spacing of your tails. Make the second cut as before, pushing the work and the angled board into the blade until the board reaches the stop. (See photo, left.) Repeat the cutting procedure to cut one side of all the

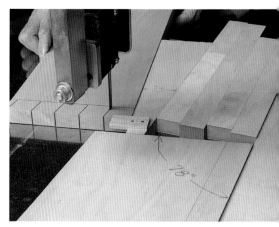

Totally spaced out. Add one spacer for each tail until you saw the last cheek.

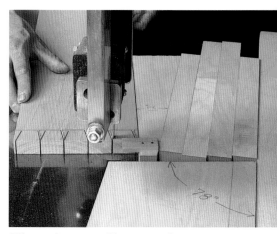

Flip and repeat. Turn over the stock and saw the opposing cheeks using the same spacers and the same cutting sequence.

cheeks, adding one spacer for each cut until you reach the last full tail, as shown in the top photo, above. Now simply flip over the stock 180° and repeat the cutting sequence on the opposing cheeks, starting with the work against the angled board and adding the same spacers in the same order until you've cut the last full tail. (See photo, above.)

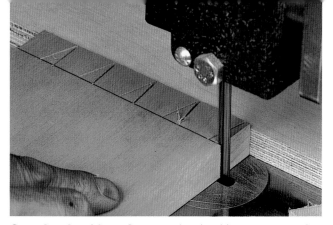

Saw the shoulders. Crosscut the shoulders square to the edge by registering the end of the work against the fence.

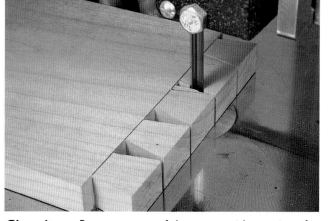

Clean it up. Remove most of the waste with a series of plunge cuts, then move the work sideways to clean up the baseline. Slender pin openings like these are possible only on the bandsaw.

Next, reset the fence and trim the shoulders to the baseline by orienting the workpiece at 90° to the blade, using the fence to guide the work. Saw each shoulder until the waste is free, as shown in the photo, above. Finally, remove the fence and freehand the stock straight into the blade to remove the waste between the cheeks, moving the work side to side to smooth and straighten the baseline. (See top right photo, above.) If necessary, use a small chisel to clean out any remaining waste in the corners.

Use the sawn tails to lay out the pins, then use a square to transfer the marks onto the inside face of the pin board. Clamp the pin-cutting jig to the saw table with one end square to and surrounding the saw blade. Clamp a straightedge to the jig at

that end, so that it stops the work when the saw blade reaches the baseline. Construct a guide block by clamping a straightedge to a square of plywood, so that the straightedge registers against the far end of the jig while the adjacent edge of the plywood is square to the blade. Now place the stock on the jig with your layout marks facing up, and use the guide block to help keep the stock square to the blade as you saw one side of each cheek. (See photo, below.)

After sawing the first round of cheeks, remove half of the waste between each cheek with a series of plunge cuts to the baseline, and by pushing the board against the stop and moving it side to side, as shown in the top left photos, opposite page.

 FIG. 5

Bandsaw Pin-Cutting Jig

Make all parts from ¾ in. plywood or MDF.

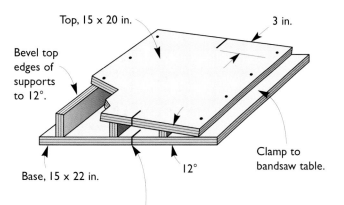

Top, 15 x 20 in.

3 in.

Bevel top edges of supports to 12°.

Clamp to bandsaw table.

Base, 15 x 22 in.

12°

Saw 3-in.-long kerf in both ends with bandsaw blade, then clamp jig to table with blade in one kerf for first series of cuts. Reverse jig on table for second round of cuts.

Tilt the work, not the table. The jig holds the work at the desired dovetail angle for sawing the pins. A moveable guide block keep the stock square to the blade as you cut the angled cheeks.

Flip the board 180° and rout the half-notch in the opposite side, aligning the opposite edge of the workpiece with the same mark you used previously. Then move the stock to the second mark, rout a full notch, and flip the board. Rout another full notch in the opposite side, again registering the work against the previous mark. Continue routing full notches in this manner until you're left with a full notch or a full tail in the center of the board. (See top left photo, next page.)

Take away half. Remove half of the waste between the cheeks by sawing straight into the baseline (top) and then moving the work sideways for a light planing cut (above).

Finish by sawing the opposing cheeks and removing the waste, reversing the jig (and its angle) in relation to the blade, with the opposite end of the jig enclosed in the blade. Make the cuts with the same face of the stock down on the jig, and repeat the cutting sequence. (See middle right photo, above.)

On the router table. You can easily and safely cut the tails on the router table using a dovetail bit and the sliding fence (see page 29). Once the tails are cut, you'll need to cut the pins with a different tool, either the table saw, bandsaw, or hand-held router. Start by scribing the baseline on the tail board; laying out the tails is unnecessary. Attach a tall zero-clearance fence to the face of the sliding fence, then adjust the bit height to the desired length of the tails. Before routing, make a series of marks on the fence that correspond to your desired tail spacing. You'll need to mark only half the total number of tails. Now clamp the stock vertically to the fence, so that one edge aligns with your first mark, and push the assembly over the bit to rout a half-notch. (See photo, right.)

Saw the opposite angle. Reposition the jig to saw the opposing cheeks and remove the waste.

Guided by lines. Stand the work against the sliding fence, aligning the edge with your marks, and push the assembly into the bit. The first cut creates a half-notch for a half-pin.

Second and third cuts. Move the workpiece to the next mark to cut a full notch, then flip the work to rout a corresponding notch at the opposite edge. A third mark registers the last pair of notches.

Blocks steady the cut. Carpet tape holds a pair of blocks to the router base, letting you slide the router over the benchtop as you trim the tails by eye with a straight bit.

With a commercial dovetail jig. Setup is similar to routing half-blind dovetails (see opposite page). The good news is that most commercial jigs will cut through-dovetails (some can't cut half-blind dovetails), and they come with the necessary dovetail bit. One drawback is that the dovetail spacing is limited by the diameter of the router bit—typically ¼ inch—so you won't be able to rout closely-spaced tails with narrow pins. Also, you can't alter the dovetail angle because it's based on the particular dovetail bit that works with the jig.

While the specific procedure for making this joint will depend on the particular jig, there are some basic methods you can follow. First, you don't need to lay out the joint; the jig's template has a series of "fingers" that takes care of aligning the bit to the workpiece. Once you've adjusted and set the fingers, you can rout both the tails and the pins with the same setup. The bit follows the fingers via a ball-bearing on the bit itself or, more typically, by a metal guide bushing attached to your router. Integral clamps hold the workpiece in the correct orientation to the bit, and the horizontal surface of the template supports the router as you make the cut.

You'll start by routing the tails, although the reverse order may be necessary, depending on the machine you're using. Install the dovetail bit in your router, and set the depth of cut to the desired dovetail length, which equals the thickness of the pin board. On most jigs, you clamp the tail board vertically in the machine, under the template. Follow the manufacturer's instructions for the specific setup and routing sequence. Rout the pins next, leaving the bit height as is. The pin board is clamped in a vertical or horizontal position, depending on the jig. Use a routing procedure similar to the one you used for the tails. Again, refer to the jig's manual to follow specific setup instructions and routing procedures.

One note: It's usually best to do a trial run on scrap stock to test the fit of the joint. If the joint is too tight or too loose, most jigs let you easily tweak the settings so you get a perfect fit in the real thing.

With a hand-held router. This is a very simple and quick method for cutting dovetail pins and involves very little setup, making it a good choice when you only have a few joints to cut. The technique relies on routing freehand, but it's not particularly difficult, and you'll get great results the first time if you follow the right setup and routing sequence. Cut the tails first, using either the table saw, bandsaw, or router table. Then use the tail board to lay out the pins on the pin board. Chuck a small-diameter straight bit in the router, and set the depth to the desired length of the pins. Attach two blocks—slightly thicker than the pin length—to the bottom of your router using double-sided (carpet) tape or screws. Position the router on the benchtop and over a bench vise, then clamp the pin board in the vise with its end contacting the bottom of the router.

Starting in the center of each waste area, rout the pins. Move the bit slowly at first to avoid blowing out the grain at the beginning of the cut. Take one full pass all the way through the stock, again slowing down as the bit exits. Then begin to widen the opening by making successive passes, pushing the router against the rotation of the bit and taking very light cuts, moving closer to the cheeks with each pass. (See photo, above.) Make a final light pass to the layout line for each cheek. On your first try, you may need to clean up the cuts with a chisel for a perfect fit. With practice, you'll be able to fit the joint directly from the router.

FIG. 6

Mitered Through-Dovetails

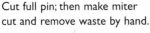
Cut full pin; then make miter cut and remove waste by hand.

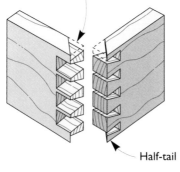

Half-tail

FIG. 7

Half-Blind Dovetails

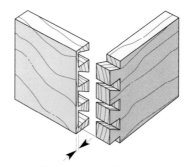

Leave $1/16$ in. or more for shoulder.

Mitered Through-Dovetails

This is the same joint as a through-dovetail, but with mitered corners at the top and bottom. The mitered detail adds an elegant touch, and it's a good joint for projects where the edges are visible, such as fine cases and small jewelry boxes. You'll need to lay out the tails and pins slightly differently here than you would with a standard through-dovetail joint, marking half-tails (instead of half-pins) at the edges of the stock. Begin with any of the approaches used for cutting a through-dovetail, then use the table saw and a little handwork to create the mitered shoulders.

On the table saw. Cut the dovetails as you would for through-dovetails (see page 140), then lay out and mark the miters on the top and bottom edges of the stock. Use the double-runner sled and a 45° fence (see page 21) to cut the miters on the tail board. Make sure to lower the blade so you don't saw into the tail above as you cut the miter below. Then lower the blade even more and use the same setup to make a shallow scoring miter cut into each half-pin on the pin board. Finish by following this shallow cut with a handsaw and chisels to remove the waste in these areas.

Half-Blind Dovetails

Another variation on the dovetail joint, half-blind dovetails are very similar to through-dovetails, except that the tails don't go all the way through on one side. This joint is excellent for joining drawer boxes, where you cut the tails in the drawer sides. The result is a very strong drawer without any visible joinery when seen from the front. Another use for half-blind dovetails is in case construction, where you need to join case corners but don't want to reveal the joint to the public. You can cut the tails using any of the methods shown for making through-dovetails (see page 140), but the pins are another matter. The best machine approach is to cut both tails and pins using a commercial dovetail jig.

With a commercial dovetail jig. No layout is necessary. The following procedure describes cutting the pins first; refer to the manufacturer's instructions for your specific jig. Install the dovetail bit in your router, and set the depth to the length of your desired tails. Remember to subtract at least $1/16$ inch for the front, or show side, of the board. Adjust the jig's template as necessary, then clamp the tail board in a vertical position, and the pin board horizontally on the top of the jig and under the template. Make sure the inside face of the pin board faces up, and the inside of the tail board faces out. Clamping the tail board at this point helps align the pin board to the jig, and allows you to rout the tails in the next step with less setup. Now rout the pins, following the fingers of the template, as shown in the top photo, next page.

Pins on top. To rout the pins, clamp the tail board vertically, then use it to help align the pin board in a horizontal position on top of the jig. Follow the fingers of the template with a guide bushing, extending the dovetail bit through the bushing.

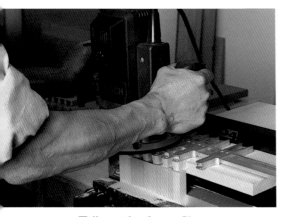

Tails at the front. Place a scrap board behind the tail board to prevent blowout, and rout the tails by turning around the template and following the fingers on its opposite side.

Cut the tails next, leaving the bit height as is. Before routing, remove the pin board and replace it with a piece of scrap. This arrangement prevents tearout on the outside, or show side, of the tails. Refer to your owner's manual for specific setup instructions. Rout the tails by following the fingers on the template of the jig, as shown in the photo, above.

Fixing a Miscut Dovetail

▶ **LET'S ADMIT IT.** Sometimes things go wrong, and we make mistakes. Cutting dovetails is no exception. The most common error is a small gap left between a tail and a pin after we've glued and assembled the joint. But it's not the end of the world; the fix is easy, as figure 8 shows. To clean out any dried glue and straighten the gap, use a fine-tooth handsaw, sawing at an angle so the blade cuts to the baseline on both sides of the joint. Then use a slip of wood to fill the gap. Veneer is an excellent choice if the gap is relatively narrow. Apply glue, and tap or push the filler piece gently into the gap. When the glue has dried, use a sharp chisel to pare the piece flush with the surrounding joint. If you take your time and do a good job, the repair will be invisible.

FIG. 8 ▶ **Filling the Gap**

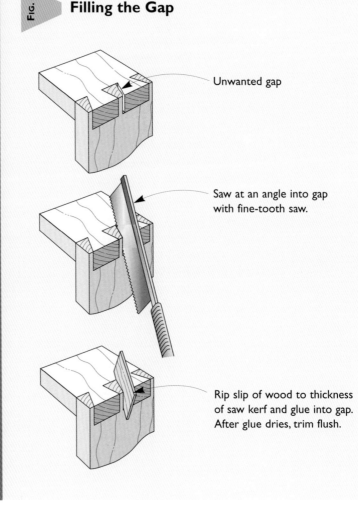

Unwanted gap

Saw at an angle into gap with fine-tooth saw.

Rip slip of wood to thickness of saw kerf and glue into gap. After glue dries, trim flush.

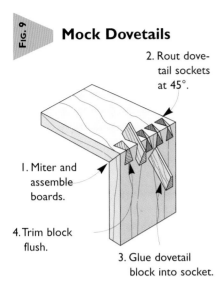

FIG. 9

Mock Dovetails

2. Rout dovetail sockets at 45°.

1. Miter and assemble boards.

4. Trim block flush.

3. Glue dovetail block into socket.

Mock Dovetails

Mock dovetails are similar in construction to the mock-finger joint (see page 89) because both joints involve adding wooden keys to a standard face-mitered corner. Here, the keys are shaped like a dovetail and are inserted into matching dovetail sockets to reinforce the miter and add a decorative detail. By using a contrasting color or species of wood for the keys, you can make this joint interesting and quite beautiful. The joint is excellent for small boxes such as jewelry or gift boxes, and looks somewhat like a through-dovetail. However, unlike a traditional dovetail, which requires careful and precise setup, the mock dovetail is relatively simple and easy to construct on the router table.

On the router table. Miter, glue, and assemble the four corners of the box. (For more on miters, see Jigs for Accurate Joints, page 20) Install a dovetail bit in the router table, and mount the work in the cradle jig (see page 30). Adjust the bit height using the same approach as you would for cutting a mock-finger joint, lining up the top of

the bit with a 45° line drawn across one of the corners of the box. This arrangement aligns the keys with the thickness of the box sides, and helps fool the eye into thinking the keys are cut from the box itself.

Rout the sockets by pushing the assembly over the bit, making sure to cut a full socket near but in from each edge of the box. You can judge the spacing of the sockets by eye if you wish, or draw a series of lines on the jig to help with aligning the work to the bit, as shown in the top photo, right.

Once all the sockets are cut, make the dovetail keys. First, prepare a length of key stock slightly thicker than the widest portion of the dovetail sockets, and wider than necessary. Remove the cradle jig and, using the same dovetail bit in the router table, clamp a fence to the table and raise the bit as high as its cutting edges will cut. Then make a pass on each side of the key stock, moving the fence in or away from the bit until the dovetail stock slips snug into a socket. (See photo, right.)

Use the bandsaw or a handsaw to cut out the individual keys, marking and cutting them oversize so they sit proud in their respective notches. (See bottom photo, right.) Apply glue and install the keys. Once the glue has dried, use the bandsaw or a handsaw to trim the excess as close to the sides of the box as possible. Then use a sharp plane to bring the keys perfectly flush to the work.

Routing through corners. Line up the edge of the box with marks drawn on the jig to gauge the spacing of the sockets. Start with a full notch near each edge.

Shape the keys. Use wide stock when routing the key blank to keep your hands clear of the bit.

Fill the sockets. Mark and cut out individual keys from the blank. Keys must be installed at 45° into the box, and should fit snug..

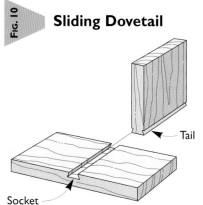

FIG. 10

Sliding Dovetail

Tail

Socket

VARIATION

Tapered Sliding Dovetail

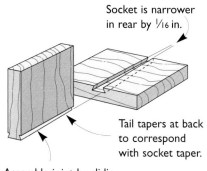

Socket is narrower in rear by 1/16 in.

Tail tapers at back to correspond with socket taper.

Assemble joint by sliding tail into socket from front.

Sliding Dovetail

The sliding dovetail is a beautiful and functional joint that offers a sound mechanical connection, making it very strong. It's used where parts intersect in the middle, such as when a divider or partition meets a case side, or when an overhanging front joins the sides of a drawer. Fitting the joint can be tricky, because the tail must mate precisely with the socket or the joint will be loose. A variation, the tapered sliding dovetail, overcomes this particular shortcoming by using a wedging effect as the joint is assembled. This makes a good fit easier to achieve, although it's more involved to make. Done successfully, this tapered joint needs little or no glue.

Rout and stop. Rout the stopped socket by guiding the edge of the router against a fence, stopping shy of the finished width of the divider.

In general, it's best to use the sliding dovetail for relatively narrow work, such as the front dividers in a case frame. Wider panels, such as shelves and partitions, are best joined with the tapered sliding dovetail. You can cut the standard sliding dovetail with a combination of the router table and a hand-held router, using the same dovetail bit in each machine. The tapered joint is cut using both tools and one dovetail bit, but with different setups.

Angle both fences. Use a square and a shim of veneer to move each fence in at the back by about 1/32 inch.

With a hand-held router. The best order of cutting is to rout the socket first, for both the standard dovetail joint and its tapered variation. Then shape the tail on the router table. To cut a straight socket for the standard joint, use a dovetail bit whose width is close to—but slightly less than—the thickness of the divider you wish to join, and install it in the router to the desired socket depth. Mark the centerline of the socket on your stock, then clamp a fence square across the work, so that the center of the bit is aligned with your mark when the router is against the fence. If you're making a stopped cut, as shown here, mark the end of the cut by transferring the width of the divider to the stock. Rout the socket in one pass, stopping the bit about 1/4 inch shy of your mark. (See top photo, above.) Be sure to switch off the router and let the bit coast to a stop before backing it out.

When routing the tapered joint, you'll need to taper the socket at the rear by about 1/16 inch. Select a dovetail bit whose width is less than the narrower area of the socket, and set it to

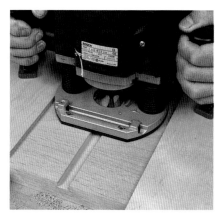

Use both sides. Follow both fences with the router, routing against the first fence and then widening the slot by following the second.

Rout the tail. Stand the work upright against a tall fence and make a pass on each side of the stock, using a wide block to steady the cut and prevent tearout.

Measure the setback. Insert the divider into the socket, and note where it stops to measure the necessary shoulder depth.

Rout it at 90°. Set the fence to the depth of the shoulder and rout the divider by orienting the stock square to the fence.

the desired socket depth. Mark the joint's centerline on the workpiece, then lightly clamp two fences square across the work and on either side of the line. The flared tip of the bit should align with each socket cheek at the front of the stock when the router is positioned against its respective fence. There should be space between the router and one fence when the router is placed against the opposite fence. Now crosscut a narrow stick of wood to fit exactly between the fences at the front of the stock, and clamp it firmly in place. At the rear of the stock, tap each fence towards the joint line, moving it about $1/32$ inch, or half the amount of taper. The best way to gauge this is to use slips of veneer as shims, placing a combination square against the back edge of the stock and the rear of the fence. Tap the fence until the veneer shim just fits between the square's blade and the front of the fence. (See bottom middle photo, opposite page.) As a last check, measure the distance between the fences at the front and at the back; the difference should be about

$1/16$ inch. Clamp both fences firmly to the stock, remove the setup stick, and set the veneer shims aside for later.

Rout the tapered notch starting at the front, pushing the router away from you and against the left fence (as it faces you). Rout through and out the back of the stock, then pull the router back towards you and against the right fence, widening the socket, as shown in the bottom right photo, opposite page.

On the router table. Once you've routed the straight socket, rout the tail in the divider using a tall fence on the router table and the same dovetail bit, adjusting the bit height to the depth of the socket. Make a test cut in scrap first, using stock of the same thickness as the divider. Stand the piece vertically on the table, and use a tall, wide block to guide the work as you push it past the bit. Make one pass on each side of the stock to form the tail, then check the fit to the socket. If it's loose, move the fence closer to the bit and rout another test tail in fresh scrap. If the joint is too tight, move the fence

away from the bit. When the test tail fits perfectly with a firm push with your hand, rout the actual divider. (See top left photo, above.)

Next, push the dovetailed divider all the way into the socket, and mark where the divider stops at the rounded ends of the socket. (See top middle photo, above.) You'll need to cut a shoulder at the back of the divider in order for its front edge to align flush with the front of the socket stock. Go back to the router table and, without changing the bit height, reset the fence to the necessary shoulder depth. Then stand the divider upright, with its back edge against the fence, and rout the shoulder, again using a push block to steer the cut, as shown in the photo, above.

To rout the tapered tail, use the same router bit and the veneer shims you used when routing the tapered socket. Attach a tall fence to the table, and set the bit height equal to the socket depth. Routing the tail is simplicity itself: Tape a veneer shim to each side of the tail stock at its front edge, then stand the work upright and guide it past the

Shims create the taper. Tape veneer shims to both sides of the stock and rout the tapered tail by making a pass on each side, making sure to place even pressure at the front and back of the board.

Tell-tale fit. A properly cut tapered sliding dovetail requires tapping to bring the last of the tail home.

bit with a push block, making one pass per side. (See top left photo, above.) As before, it's wise to test your setup on scrap, moving the fence into the bit if the fit is too loose, or away from the bit to tighten the joint. You can tell when the fit is precise: Assemble the joint by sliding the tail piece into the socket from the front. It should slide easily into place, then begin to tighten. You should have to tap the last 1 inch or so of the tail with light blows from a hammer, as shown in the photo, left.

FIG. 2

Dovetail Keys

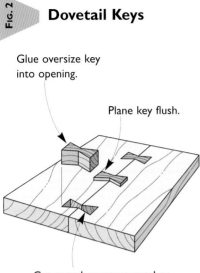

Glue oversize key into opening.

Plane key flush.

Cut complementary notches in adjoining boards.

Dovetail Keys

Dovetail keys, also known as butterfly keys, can be inlaid into a panel wherever two long-grain edges meet, such as in a standard butt joint. The keys' distinctive shape adds visual charm and a mechanical connection to the joint, and can be used on a variety of panel projects, from tabletops and doors to serving trays and other flat surfaces. For extra appeal, you can make the keys from a contrasting color or species of wood. The joint is best made on the router table.

On the router table. Prepare straight and smooth edges as you would a standard edge-to-edge butt joint (see page 43). You'll cut the dovetail notches before gluing up the panel. To do this, install a dovetail bit in the router table and raise it to one-half of the desired key length. Then mount the sliding fence (see page 29) on the router table. Position the two boards face to face and clamp them to the fence, with

their prepared edges on the table. The setup is similar to routing the tails for through-dovetails (see page 140). Rout a pair of complementary sockets in one pass, pushing the work over the bit. If the desired key is wider than the bit you're using, simply move the stock sideways and make a second pass to widen the sockets. Repeat on the appropriate areas of the boards if you're inlaying more than one key.

Next, rout the dovetail keys. First, on a nearby bench, clamp the two boards edge-to-edge, and measure the butterfly-shaped opening. Prepare a key blank to the exact length and width of the opening. Measure the width at the widest part of the dovetail. Be careful to orient the blank so the grain runs across the opening and at 90° to the grain of the panel. This orientation ensures strong keys. Remove the sliding fence, and install a router fence equipped with a zero-clearance fence on the router table. Reset the dovetail bit height to precisely one-half the height of the blank, and make four passes, turning the stock 180° and end-for-end, to rout all four areas of the blank. (See top right photo, above.)

Rip individual keys from the blank on the table saw or bandsaw, making them slightly thicker than the panel. (See photo, right.) Glue up the panel, then apply glue to the keys tap them into the openings, leaving them slightly proud. When the glue has dried, finish the joint by leveling the keys with a few strokes from a sharp plane.

Making butterflies. Use a zero-clearance fence, and orient the grain of the blank facing up as shown. Four passes, using a push stick with each pass, create the distinctive butterfly shape.

Slice n' serve. Rip individual keys from the blank, then glue them into the dovetailed openings. Plane the keys flush once the glue has dried.

Gallery

▲ **John Babot**
Cabinet
Koa and jarrah; dowels, dadoes, rabbets, and tongue-and-groove.
Photos by David Welter

◄ **Frank Klausz**
Hepplewhite corner cabinet
Mahogany, mahogany crotch veneer, satinwood, ebony, and holly; mitered butt joints, dadoes, rabbets, tongue-and-groove, mortise-and-tenon, and mitered half-laps.
Photo by Bill Prouty

▶ Ejler Hjorth-Westh
Game table
Mahogany, redwood-lace burl, Carpathian elm, wenge, and ebony; biscuits, loose tenons, and half-blind dovetails.
Photo by Kevin Shea

▼ Yeung Chan
Jewelry box
Birch plywood and walnut; compound-splined miters, splined miters, and tongue-and-groove.
Photos by Steve Burns

◀ Ejler Hjorth-Westh
Dining chair
Bubinga and leather; loose tenons.
Photo by Kevin Shea

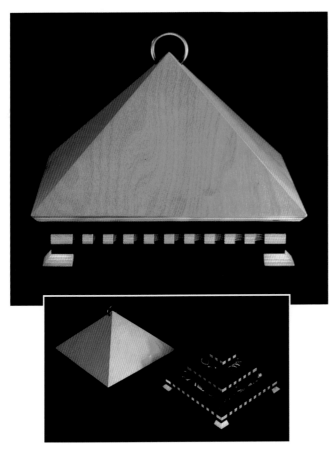

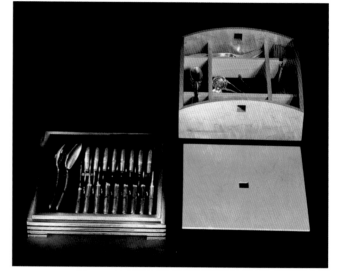

▲ Yeung Chan
Silverware box
Maple, walnut, and birch plywood; splined miters,
half-laps, and tongue-and-groove.
Photo by Steve Burns

◄ Yeung Chan
Display cabinet
Kwila and maple; dowels, rabbets, tongue-and-groove,
half-blind dovetails, through-dovetails, half-laps, and mul-
tiple-tenon slip joints.
Photo by Seth Janofsky

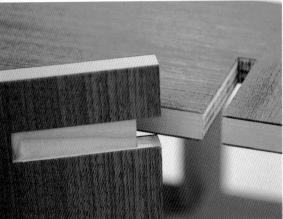

▲ **Armin Driver**
Knock-down end table
Doussie and guatambu; unglued edge-laps.
Photos by David Welter

◀ **Ejler Hjorth-Westh**
Dining table and captain's chair
Bubinga and leather; loose tenons, key-dovetailed laps,
edge-to-edge butt joints, and dowels.
Photo by Kevin Shea

► **Vajra Ricci**
Blanket chest
Douglas fir and mahogany;
edge-to-edge spline joints,
tongue-and-groove, mortise-
and-tenon, and dadoes.
Photo by David Welter

▼ **Ejler Hjorth-Westh**
Sideboard
Pear, pear veneer, bubinga, and
bubinga veneer; biscuits, tongue-
and-groove, slip joints, rabbets,
mortise-and-tenon, half-blind
dovetails, and through-dovetails.
Photo by Kevin Shea

▲ **Frank Klausz**
Frank and Edith's kitchen
Cherry and maple plywood;
biscuits, dadoes, rabbets, and
through-wedged tenons.
Photo by Sandor Nagyszalanczy

▲ **Kevin Drake**
Jewelry box
Spanish cedar with ebony splines; through-splined
miters, mortise-and-tenon, and tongue-and-groove.
Photo by David Welter

◄ **J.T. Scott**
Display cabinet
Kwila and maple; dowels, slip joints, and half-laps.
Photo by David Welter

▲ **Isaiah Abbatiello**
Tea box
Cherry and moabi; splined miters, dadoes,
and mortise-and-tenon.
Photos by David Welter

◄ **Margaret O'Brien**
Cabinet on stand
Pear; dowels and mortise-and-tenon.
Photos by David Welter

◀ **Jennifer Anderson**
Bench
Wenge; mortise-and-tenon
and dowels.
Photo by David Welter

▶ **Paul Lynch**
Table
Curly maple; through-wedged
tenons, mortise-and-tenon, and
edge-to-edge butt joints.
Photo by David Welter

◄ **William McArthur**
End tables
Walnut; mortise-and-tenon, rabbets, half-blind dovetails, and through-dovetails.
Photo by Mark Saffron

▼ **Frank Klausz**
Lowboy
Curly maple and white pine; haunched mortise-and-tenon, dadoes, rabbets, half-blind dovetails, through-dovetails, and tapered sliding dovetails.
Photos by Bill Prouty

◄ **Carl Zytowski**
Chest of drawers
Bubinga and white oak; dowels,
mortise-and-tenon, rabbets,
half-blind dovetails, and
through-dovetails.
Photos by David Welter

◀ **Adrian Ferrazzutti**
Chair
Hickory and leather; multiple
through-wedged tenons.
Photos by David Welter

◄ **William McArthur**
End table
Pear and maple; dowels, dadoes,
rabbets, and half-laps.
Photo by Jeff Odee

▶ **Brad Bielka**
Music box
Pear and rosewood;
through-dovetails, mortise-and-
tenon, and tongue-and-groove.
Photos by David Welter

▲ **William McArthur**
Nesting coffee tables
Rosewood and pear; splined
miters and tongue-and-groove.
Photos by Jay Odee

◀ **Yeung Chan**
Wall cabinet
Ash; dowels, rabbets, half-laps, tongue-and-groove,
and bridle lap joints.
Photo by Yeung Chan

▶ **Kevin Mitchell**
Clock
Rosewood and Douglas fir;
dowels and tongue-and-groove.
Photo by David Welter

◀ **Yeung Chan**
Flower stand
Doussie; splined miters,
dovetailed tongue-and-groove, and mortise-and-tenon.
Photos by Seth Janofsky

Metric Conversion Table

Inches	Centimeters	Inches	Centimeters
1/8	3 mm	12	30
1/4	6 mm	13	32.5
3/8	9 mm	14	35
1/2	1.3	15	37.5
5/8	1.6	16	40
3/4	1.9	17	42.5
7/8	2.2	18	45
1	2.5	19	47.5
1 1/4	3.1	20	50
1 1/2	3.8	21	52.5
1 3/4	4.4	22	55
2	5	23	57.5
2 1/2	6.25	24	60
3	7.5	25	62.5
3 1/2	8.8	26	65
4	10	27	67.5
4 1/2	11.3	28	70
5	12.5	29	72.5
5 1/2	13.8	30	75
6	15	31	77.5
7	17.5	32	80
8	20	33	82.5
9	22.5	34	85
10	25	35	87.5
11	27.5	36	90

Index

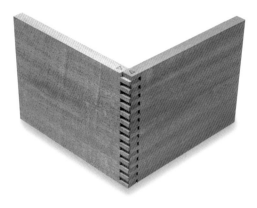

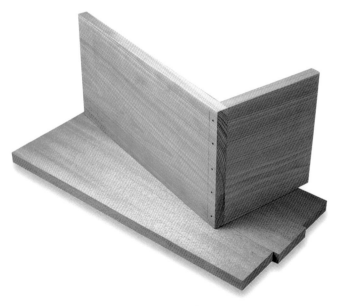

"Cutting accurate joints means using accurate power tools."